THE
MONEY
MAKERS

THE
MONEY
MAKERS

*Six portraits of
power in industry*

DAVID LOMAX

BBC PUBLICATIONS

This book accompanies the BBC Television
series *The Money Makers* first broadcast on
BBC 2 from February 1986 and repeated on
BBC 1 from September 1986.

The series was produced by Brian Davies.

Published to accompany a series of
programmes prepared in consultation with
the BBC Continuing Education Advisory
Council.

Published by BBC Publications,
a division of BBC Enterprises Ltd
35 Marylebone High Street, London W1M 4AA

First published 1986
ISBN: 0 563 21276 4

Typeset in 11/13.5 point Palatino Roman by
Oxford Publishing Services, Oxford
Printed and bound in Great Britain by
Mackays of Chatham Ltd

Photographic credits (front cover):
Top left by Camera Press Limited,
all others by David Lomax

Illustrations by David E. Smith.

CONTENTS

ACKNOWLEDGEMENTS

I am grateful to our producer, Dr Brian
Davies, of BBC TV's Continuing Education
Department, and to his researcher, Elizabeth
Farrar. Without their enthusiasm and
diplomacy the original series would not have
been filmed; without their help and
encouragement this book would not have
been written.

My thanks are also due to Steve Vines of the
Observer and Gualberto Ranieri of Fiat for
advice, and to Godfrey Johnson, Martyn
Clift, Arthur Chesterman, Henry Farrar,
Clare O'Donovan, Shelley Hirst, Jim Wilson
and Alex Richardson for their filming skills
and good-humoured support.

Finally, I am grateful to my wife, Judy, for
her professional help.

INTRODUCTION

It is said – too often perhaps – that travel broadens the mind. Having done a lot of it in my time I am not so sure about the broadening; lengthening might be a better description, or stretching, even pummelling. The effect of the different kaleidoscope of impressions which flying across many different countries has on a wilting passenger is, in some people, a theoretical tendency to turn everything into mournful and uniform grey.

When we left Britain to film the BBC TV Continuing Education series on which this book is based, we had a magnificent opportunity to put this travelling theory to its ultimate test. Could we survive and keep our mental colour vision intact and fresh? We were to fly round the world interviewing six of the most important businessmen in their different countries, one after the other. The expedition had to be undertaken at high pressure for reasons of economy, and this heightened the kaleidoscopic effect.

On one day, for instance, we were flying high over the New Mexican desert in Robert Anderson's private jet, listening to his account of the latest deals in Peking; a couple of days later we were on the bullet express in Japan with Mr Akio Morita, the head of Sony, who enthusiastically demonstrated a new electronic toy which he just happened to have in his briefcase. We could compare the experience of flying with Giovanni Agnelli in a Fiat helicopter over his car factories in Turin with what it was like to follow the head of Tata Steel, Mr Russi Mody, around a vast plant in the middle of the poorest state in India, or to ride in the back of Mr Stanley Ho's third Rolls Royce in Hong Kong and ask him about the millions he has made from a string of casinos. In the end, I suppose, there was not much danger that a series of vivid experiences and comparisons could ever be grey. I hope we were able to convey some of its powerful colour to our TV audience.

The idea for a series of documentary film portraits of leading businessmen came about because of Britain's so-called 'Industry Year'. The programmes were intended to provoke discussion about Britain's apparent bias against all matters industrial, and about what could or should be done to rescue our manufacturing industries and improve management in general. Six international businessmen agreed to take part. Their names were chosen after considerable research, debate and diplomacy by producer Brian Davies and researcher Elizabeth Farrar from a shortlist of significant possibilities. They were all of international stature, good speakers, colourful personalities who knew Britain well and who had important and relevant things to say about our current condition.

Not everyone we asked approved of our intentions and some had other commitments. Some industrialists evidently thought their businesses might suffer if they exposed themselves to the risk of making a damaging slip in a frank conversation; others obviously thought our proposal was a chance for the skilful moulding of some free publicity. We were conscious throughout of the delicate balance between the extreme of advertising and exposé. I hope we managed to walk the tightrope successfully and with an open mind.

We are all very grateful to the six men who eventually agreed to take part in the *Money Makers* series. They all gave us more of their time than they were obliged to do and were co-operative and friendly. I apologise that no woman was included in the programmes: perhaps this will be remedied in a future series.

It was a gruelling challenge to make these films one after the other, but at least it gave us a unique chance to compare our subjects at close range. The result is not, of course, some glib magic formula for making money – the chemistry of successful international business on this scale is far too complex and elusive for that. But there are other lessons which I hope will be even more important and more interesting.

For myself, I found that the chance of talking to some of

the world's most successful businessmen was an enjoyable and illuminating experience. Each is, of course, an inevitable product of his own background, but, at the same time, far more than a representative of a single national success story. All have relevant comments to make about Britain as well as about their own countries, and all of them draw internationally relevant conclusions. Many of their observations are not concerned with Britain's 'Industry Year', but, as the first of our subjects, Sir John Harvey-Jones of ICI, has pointed out, industry in Britain, as elsewhere, should not confine its efforts to a single year. Perhaps his comment that 'In Japan every year is an Industry Year' should be taken to heart.

David Lomax
July 1986

SIR JOHN HARVEY~JONES OF ICI

CHAPTER 1

THE SUBMARINER
WHO KEPT ICI AFLOAT

High above the roaring London traffic, in one of a row of walnut-panelled offices with ponderous furniture and uniformed tea ladies, Sir John Harvey-Jones, the Chairman of Imperial Chemical Industries, plans his revolutionary strategy, intent on streamlining the company and ridding it of its image of being mighty and unchanging. At one time he even hinted that he would like to close the ICI building opposite the Houses of Parliament, and move the company's headquarters somewhere more in keeping with the role of the lean and thrusting organisation he was trying to create: Neo-Grecian corridors may be culturally civilised, but he felt that they had 'bugger all to do with running a business'. In the event this removal proved too difficult and too revolutionary to effect.

So ICI still overlooks the Houses of Parliament: it will, if Sir John's ambitions for its future are realised, no doubt continue to be the barometer of the country's economic health long after Britain's most outspoken and best known businessman, with his piratical long hair, loud ties and open criticism of Margaret Thatcher's government, has gone down in company history as its most colourful Chairman. Even his natural opponents in the unions, angered by his ruthless pruning of jobs and policy of investing outside Britain, praise his 'charisma' and comment favourably on his relaxed and informal attitude and appearance.

To the average passer-by, the formal Portland stone office block of monumental proportions which gazes confidently over Millbank and the Thames appears to be merely another British institution. The headquarters of the chemical giant, ICI, is the nerve centre of an organisation with more than 500 subsidiaries in forty different countries. It makes everything from paint to plastics, polythene buckets to pesticides, perspex, polyester fabrics and beta-blocker heart drugs, and exports goods from Britain worth, it is claimed, a million pounds every working hour.

Imperial Chemical Industries was conceived after the First World War when four British firms amalgamated to challenge German and American chemical competition more effectively. The deal was struck in October 1926 aboard the liner Aquitania in mid-Atlantic. A typed agreement on Cunard notepaper recorded how Sir Harry McGowan, Chairman of Nobel Industries, and Sir Alfred Mond, Chairman of Brunner, Mond, two of Britain's leading chemical manufacturers, agreed over lunch to form a defensive alliance against foreign competition and take over two smaller businesses, the British Dyestuffs Corporation and the United Alkali Company. The new company was launched with a share capital of £65 million, and was called Imperial because it was to trade with the British Empire. The name was later thought unfashionable, even undesirable, but by then ICI was so well established that it was decided not to change it.

ICI, after some initial uncertainties, gradually prospered. At the same time it was the first major British company to give shares to the workers and to introduce works' councils. It invented perspex and polythene in the thirties, and in the Second World War had government contracts to produce explosives, propellants and even poisonous gas – which was never used. After the war the company continued to expand and became one of the recognised pillars of Britain's industrial establishment. Its share performance mirrored the nation's economic health. In its sober headquarters, regiments of respectable grey men whose names were unknown to the nation wielded, in concert, immense industrial power.

Eventually these men became institutionalised in the success of the company they had established. As markets changed, ICI was not able to adapt. In times of continuing expansion its inefficiencies were generally masked, but when the oil crisis broke, over-manning and bureaucracy had a stranglehold on progress. A crisis gradually crept upon a self-satisfied company which for many years had either chosen to ignore or simply had not noticed the signs. ICI allowed itself to become grossly over-manned; it failed to exploit world markets, believing that home and Commonwealth markets were sufficient, and failed to see that the recession of the mid-seventies would mean over-production of the cheaper plastics, fibres and chemicals to which it was already heavily committed.

In 1982, when John Harvey-Jones took over as Chairman, the unthinkable had happened: in the second half of 1980, ICI had suffered the shock and humiliation of its first post-war losses. Dividends were cut for the first time in the company's history. The appointment was a gamble by the ICI board: John Harvey-Jones had neither spent his working life in the organisation, nor was he a trained scientist. It could be interpreted as almost a move of desperation, since ICI was in such trouble that it was realised that something revolutionary was needed: 'Maybe they thought it was better to take a big risk, and thought that I was indeed a big risk,' Sir John told us, adding: 'I think I still am a big risk, incidentally.'

He undoubtedly had the force of personality to impose controversial and painful measures, and it was this ability which mattered most. Within four years he had rescued the company. He reorganised it, closed inefficient plant and streamlined management. The process started at the top, where the board was cut from eighteen to eight members, and continued through every level. The reporting procedures between boardroom and shop floor, which at one time had involved 160 people, were ruthlessly pruned, and many committees were scrapped. Managers were encouraged to delegate as much as possible and to release talent at junior levels. When ICI determined to switch investment into the new speciality chemical markets and to cut expenditure in the bulk chemical loss-making plants at home, thousands of workers and management were made redundant.

In less than four years this harsh medicine brought results. The share price doubled and ICI became the first company in Britain with an annual profit of more than a billion pounds. Sir John earned the reputation of being the most successful and the best known businessman in Britain. In keeping with a new policy that ICI should adopt a high public profile, he was also considered the most unusual businessman in the country. It was noticed in Fleet Street and beyond that he cultivated long hair and loud ties, did not support the Conservative Party (he has been called one of the most prominent supporters of the SDP) and was not shy about appearing on radio and television.

When one meets him one is immediately struck by his almost piratical flowing hair and bushy eyebrows, and by his apparent pride in speaking as directly as he can. There are no phrases wrapped in pleasantries and no obvious ambiguities. He does not believe in subtleties of speech, but says what he means: 'I wasn't implying: I don't think I usually imply,' he told me testily in answer to a question about the evidence he gave to a House of Lords' Select Committee on Overseas Trade in April 1985. He is a big man, who obviously has a healthy appetite and does not look as if he gets enough exercise. Always ready, it seems, to enjoy a hostile question and go on the offensive, he has a loud barking voice when he wants to make himself heard, but a surprisingly nervous-sounding laugh. Large soft hands hide a cramped and jerky handwriting style in which his pen seems to twitch of its own volition.

Throughout our interview, he glared at us with steely blue eyes which rarely changed expression, whether he was talking about his present role in British business or his extraordinary early life in a Maharaja's palace in India. His father was hired to administer the state and act as the guardian of an under-age Maharajah, and he spent his earliest years growing up with 'a sort of surrogate brother' about five or six years older than himself, surrounded by all the trappings and splendour of a Maharajah's palace in the India of the British Empire. At the age of five, the State Band played 'Happy Birthday' to him outside the marble palace: not much more than a year later his mother brought him back to England and, as he put it, dumped him in a preparatory school in Kent before herself returning to India.

At his prep. school, which he hated, he felt that he was considered something of an outcast, different from the other boys because he had neither a home, nor even a background in England, and knew nothing about the country's geography: 'I was just an oddball, a sort of Mowgli.' He was constantly aware that he fell far short of the standards set by his father, who had played rugger for England, was a first class shot, and was 'everyone's beau ideal: anything he took up in a sporting way he was brilliant at.' Sir John says that he was in comparison 'an absolute duffer at everything except swimming – and I could shoot. Those were the only two actual abilities I had.'

He compensated for his lack of sporting success by developing a passionate and escapist interest in reading. His early years in India had left him ill prepared for English school life, but his resulting sense of isolation and escape into schoolboy novels left him with an enduring love of reading and 'an ability to work extremely hard and concentrate': because he had started so far behind, he felt that he had to apply himself to achieve any standards comparable to those of the other boys. It also gave him an ability 'to endure and to take extremes of personal misery', although he admits that to say so would would hurt his late headmaster: 'I mean, even now, I can barely describe how totally desolate I felt at that school . . . there's been no period of my life when I've felt more unhappy.'

His voracious prep. school appetite for Henty, Percy Westerman and Captain W.E.Johns gave him a romantic schoolboy vision of the world which led him to think of a life in the Navy. His family on both sides had a military tradition, and it was considered natural, in a family like his, for the children to be educated in England and then to proceed to some form of public service life. The decision to opt for the Navy had, he told us, to be made at the age of ten: the Dartmouth entrance exam, which was slightly different from the public school Common Entrance of the time, required 'some special cramming'.

When the young John Harvey-Jones wrote to his parents to tell them of his wish to join the Navy, they in turn wrote round to all the family. In spite of a certain amount of initial dissent – the family tradition was Army rather than Navy – on the basis that joining any one of the services was better than some of the other terrible things he might have chosen to do, he was given their joint permission.

Whereas he had been miserable at his prep. school, he

found Dartmouth 'absolutely fantastic', although he describes the discipline as 'absolutely draconian, really draconian. I mean they flogged boys. . . but it was fair.' He avoided flogging, but 'got beaten a number of times'. It was, in retrospect, 'a super life', in spite of, or perhaps even because of, the discipline. 'I loved the discipline,' he told us, 'it had a degree of certainty about it and the whole thing just fitted with me.' He believed totally that he was privileged to be there, lucky to have the chance of being an officer in what he was 'totally convinced' was the finest navy in the world: 'Indeed at that time not only was it the finest – and it seems difficult to imagine that there can be such a change in a lifetime – but it was also the largest navy in the world by a substantial margin.'

He was twelve when he went to the Royal Naval College at Dartmouth, where he learnt self-reliance, a sense of values, and 'simple things' like punctuality and precision, and at the same time found the security for which he craved. By the time he was seventeen he had gone to sea as a midshipman during the war. He was twice torpedoed in destroyers which sank under him, and eventually decided to volunteer for submarines, in which he served until the end of the war. One of the attractions of a submarine was for him that 'either everybody went, or nobody went': it was 'a sort of clean life and clean death'. Although he joked about it, he felt that, since the enemy seemed determined to sink him, he might as well start under the water in the first place, and that might 'help a bit'.

After the war, John Harvey-Jones volunteered for a six-month Russian course at Cambridge – he had already learned German at Dartmouth – and then joined Naval Intelligence. Although he does not speak of what he had to do when appointed as a Naval Intelligence adviser to Number 10, Downing Street, his knowlege of Russian was presumably relevant. He does however admit to having served for a time in the Baltic as the peace-time skipper of an E Boat: its role was 'fishery protection'. We were told that we could read into that whatever we liked: it brought him the award of the MBE in 1952.

In 1947 John Harvey-Jones married a Wren, Betty Bignell.

When their only daughter, Gabby, contracted polio in 1955, he decided he needed more time with his family and resigned from the Navy: 'The Navy was a super job but it was no good for a married man. I mean, I'd been away for something like three years on the trot. After my daughter was born, I saw her, I think, for six weeks until she was three.' He felt that he needed to be at home and wanted what he thought would be a nine-to-five job: 'I thought there was going to be an economic problem in the United Kingdom, and therefore I wanted to join an industry which was basic rather than something which I thought was more at risk.'

His brother-in-law was in ICI, and two of his colleagues from Naval Intelligence had recently joined the company. So, when the Navy agreed to release him on compassionate grounds, he applied to ICI: to his great surprise, he was taken on, which meant a considerable cut in pay. His initial salary of £800, as a works study officer at Wilton on Teeside, was in fact half what he had been earning: 'industry was rough in tooth and claw, much tougher than the services'. He and his wife had worked out how little they could live on for two years, and when he was asked what pay he expected – 'which was a pretty dirty trick, but that's what I was asked' – he gave the figure they had arrived at. As his prospective employer wrote down the amount, 'a look of excited expectancy flashed across his eyes': that, of course, was what he was offered as a starting salary.

The Harvey-Jones's had thought that within two years either he would demonstrate his true worth and be paid accordingly, or, if he was not 'moving satisfactorily', they would have to move somewhere else where they could 'make out': 'but it proved to be a fatal mistake because we had a very complicated pay system in those days, which all depended on what you started at: any pay rise you got when you were promoted, you got a little bit immediately and the rest in increments over five years.' It was not until he joined the board that he was paid on the basis of equality.

Although financially it took him a long time to catch up, Sir John's progression on ICI's promotional ladder was relentless. After his appointment in 1956 as a works study officer on

Teeside, he was soon organising whole plants, although his enthusiasm was occasionally not appreciated. When he had the bright idea, on Teeside, of selling ICI's own petrol, which was a byproduct from one of the big distillation processes, he was hauled over the coals by the Board because he had not asked permission to use the ICI logo on the new petrol stations. His London bosses were adamant that the logo could not be used, and he had to have it removed: selling petrol was too far removed from the normal image of chemical production. ICI petrol was slightly cheaper than other brands and sold well: it is now sold in many parts of the north of England under the ICI logo, just as he had intended.

As well as starting ICI petrol, John Harvey-Jones ran a whole division and, in 1973, was elected to the main ICI board at the age of forty-nine. Five years later, he was made a Deputy Chairman. He had been moved so often within the company that when, as Chairman, he was guest of the week on *Desert Island Discs*, Roy Plomley asked him whether giving him a different job every year had been 'a desperate attempt by ICI to find something he could do'.

His own assessment of why he had been given the top job was that, when the company clearly needed to change – 'it was not performing well and had already tried doing what it had been doing before' – it was well known that he stood for change. It was not because he did not come from a technological background that he considered himself a risk, but because he wanted to change everything at once – 'and that's a very big risk'. He wanted moreover to make very big changes and did not believe that there was enough time to do things in an evolutionary way. His style was, as he described it to us, to believe very much in informality and frankness, as well as in quite a high level of conflict: 'I believe in doing things together; I believe in collective leadership – I don't think anyone's clever enough to take all the decisions on his own. I think you should heighten difference rather than smother it; I believe in minimal levels, smaller groups, very short lines of communication.' It all sounded rather like a businessman's version of the Creed.

In his ideal company, which would be a federation of free men working together of their own free will to achieve a common aim, he would like to hold a mirror up to the company so that everyone could align themselves in it: 'I don't believe that you achieve that by sending down detailed directives and saying, "No. 22 shuffle up a bit or No. 16 shuffle back".' It is, he is convinced, better to have clear objectives and 'leave the absolute maximum amount to the individuals who have to do it to do themselves'.

By 'a high level of conflict', he said he meant that he did not like to see differences concealed in 'ritual dancing and formulae': 'I think it's better that you should say "I want to go to A" and I shall say "I think you're bananas, we've plainly got to go to B", and we should argue about it openly.' He does not think this is 'adversarial', but defines it rather as a question of 'exploring areas of difference and differences of opinion in order to arrive at something which all sides can support and which, hopefully, will be better than any individual view'.

He demands of others a sense of commitment and a dedication to a joint aim as great as his own, and sees part of his role as 'persuading people to accept that aim and to put quite extraordinary efforts into the achievement of it.' ICI is, as he reminded us, 'a voluntary force: nobody can be forced to work for ICI'. 'I don't have the naval discipline act behind me,' he told us, 'I can fire people but that's not the point. It's very very easy to fire people but that's a negative thing. What I've got to do is to have willing people who believe in what we're trying to do and dedicate themselves to trying to do it. It's a switch on, not a switch off.'

His first requirement of his managers, and of himself, is toughness, both physical and mental: 'Without it, you can't do these jobs. They are absolutely grinding; the sheer physical demands in terms of hours, the ability to stay with them, the ability not to panic under pressure, the ability to try to be continuously in control of your decisions, to be able to face the nasty consequences of some decisions and take them, are all elements which are absolutely essential. Without those you haven't got anything.' When he looks around at most success-ful people, he sees toughness as the single common factor, although there are of course many other qualities he considers desirable, such as good judgement and the ability to communicate both in writing and in words, 'which enables people to give of their best to achieve a common aim'.

To an outsider, there might seem little difference between Sir John's definition of toughness and ruthlessness. When I put this to him, he admitted 'I'm rather regretting having used the word toughness now,' and rephrased his answer in an effort to make absolutely sure that I understood the point he was making: 'First of all you need sheer physical ability to keep going. You have to be able to work long hours, to concentrate and to lead an incredibly unhealthy life and keep doing it.' He is a self-confessed example: he normally starts work at six in the morning and seldom gets to sleep before one or two. 'If you actually wanted an unhealthy life, the life of a leading businessman is just about as unhealthy as you can have,' he told us, 'I don't have to, but I do eat caviar and chips at lunchtime and dinner twice a day. I'm invariably entertaining; I drink and am offered drinks the whole time; I'm whisked from here to there by cars, by aeroplanes; I stagger to my feet and walk a few yards from time to time.'

It is a life he nevertheless intends to continue leading at least until the end of his term of office as Chairman, because he is a businessman and 'achievement orientated', and because he believes 'desperately' in his company: 'I believe that the company deserves every single thing I can give it; that's what I can give it and that's what I do give it.' Even so, he needs to relax sometimes and deliberately compartmentalises his life. Since his appointment, he told us, he had had only four business telephone calls at home: he insists on keeping his home life separate, and business associates, colleagues and employees know that they should only ring him at home if there is something that only he can do and which cannot possibly be put off. 'That's why I have a private life,' he explained. 'When I get home I drop things like a brick. I never work at home; I never open a paper at home.' His public life is inflicted as little as possible on his wife, and he has made a conscious decision not to indulge in his free time in activities in which she does not wish to join: she does not, for instance, enjoy sailing, and so, although he says that when he retires he may resume his interest in this sport, at the moment he stays on land.

At home, at the weekends and sometimes in the evening during the week, he often cooks for the family – his daughter and grandchild live with him and his wife. Somehow he finds time to read at least two novels or non-work books a week: he says that he is incapable of going to sleep without reading something, even if it is only a page. Whenever possible, he swims every day in his private pool and, although he does not consider himself an expert, derives 'a tremendous pleasure' from the countryside, relaxing by watching birds and driving a donkey and trap. His donkey, which he describes as magnificent, 'a sort of superdonk', has also been driven, although only once, by Harvey Smith: 'so you can tell he's a pretty good classy donkey'. Driving has a particular fascination for him 'because you can only drive by being in the mind of the animal, and you have very few aids, very little control on the animal, and you've only got your voice'. Donkeys are, he considers, very intelligent: 'they will only do what you can chat them up to do.' He did not volunteer any comment about whether he feels that this also applies to people.

After the disastrous results of 1980 ICI was receptive to the straightforward, no-nonsense style of the remedies John Harvey-Jones proposed. The unions, too, grudgingly recognised that there was a positive side to the changes management brought about, in spite of the accompanying loss of jobs, although some were cautious about giving all the credit for the improvements to one man. Mr Roger Lyons, the Chemical Officer of the ASTMS, for instance, said that Sir John could not be held wholly responsible for the successes of the company, and cited the examples of pharmaceuticals and ICI's extension into the North Sea, both of which, he said, had been brought about by others. He admitted that ICI's most flamboyant chairman was 'a very charismatic personality who has achieved a lot in a short time', but told us that this had both a positive and a negative side: 'Speaking for the workforce of ICI, I see a lot more of the negative side than perhaps others do.' Mr Lyons told us that although he did not wish to criticise Sir John's style of 'mixing it with journalists and trade union officials, and on first name terms', this friendly and informal approach meant that 'while they're having the knife of unemployment put in between their shoulder blades, he's buying you a drink at the bar'.

The number of redundancies at ICI has been a serious concern for the unions. Morale in petrochemicals is rock bottom, according to Mr Lyons, who claims that there is particular resentment about the way the new Chairman closed the club houses and social facilities. 'The paternalistic side of ICI is not just being eroded, but hacked away,' we were told. This process is seen by many union officials as a betrayal of those who have sacrificed their working lives to make the company great. 'South of Watford, in the City, they have a very positive view of the company – its profits, its billion pounds. The City has ranked ICI as a growth company,' Mr Lyons said, 'but North of Watford it is a different story. Sir John Harvey-Jones is seen as the human face of the dole queue. These communities, dominated by ICI, are Sir John's responsibility. You can't run a major British institution that has had hundreds of millions of taxpayers' money in grants and loans over the years, and have that company internationalise itself at the direct expense of the communities that made it all possible.'

Sir John declined to comment on how he was regarded by the unions at ICI: that was something we'd better ask them, he said, as he would not presume to judge for himself how they saw him. But he knew how he would like to be regarded: as someone who believes in unions and who is fair, tough and truthful, and concerned – concerned, above everything. He said that he was, however, not surprised, only sad, that Mr Roger Lyons of the ASTMS had called him the human face of the dole queue, although he claimed not to be totally sure what this meant. 'My job,' he reiterated, 'is to run a successful company, and the job of this company is to create the wealth without which the whole of our society cannot survive.' Somebody, he maintained, had to pay this country's way in the world, and that task was the lot of manufacturing industry, within which he felt himself to have 'an absolute obligation' – to ensure that his company survives for a hundred years at least after he leaves. That, he said, could be done only by ensuring that it was 'totally competitive', which meant that he could not afford to employ a single man more on a job than his competitors did: 'I am not setting the race, but I cannot opt out of it.'

He felt it to be 'a con' and 'untrue and unfair' – 'and our people know better than that' – to try to pretend that it was within his gift to employ more people and opt out of the competitive race, because all that would happen would be that 'You may survive for a few years, but ultimately the whole lot goes.' This left him with no alternative, he explained: 'So what we have to do is to be competitive, but if we are competitive we have to try and look after and help those who leave us, and we have to try to deal with those who work with us in an understanding and fair and concerned way.' North of Watford, thousands have lost their jobs in order that ICI can be competitive, but he told us that he felt his approach was nevertheless accepted there: 'Most of our people work in the North East and the North West, and they have every opportunity to tell me if they think I am acting irresponsibly. I sense tremendous support and a great deal of understanding.'

Even Roger Lyons, who is not alone in feeling that Sir John 'is able to draw people to him with a certain degree of warmth, while at the same time making decisions which are extremely cruel and hurt a lot of people', agrees that he is more willing than most in British industry to to be open and involve the trade union representatives. But he also believes that because of his warmth Sir John 'has conned quite a few people', while at the same time policies have been implemented which have not been in the interest of ICI employees, their families and communities: 'There are areas like Teeside and Runcorn that are mere shells now, living examples of this policy.' He called Teeside 'an area of disaster' and claimed that 'These communities dominated by ICI are Harvey-Jones' responsibility'.

Wilton on Teeside is the setting of one of a number of huge and expensive errors to which Sir John Harvey-Jones is openly prepared to admit. These were probably inevitable in a vast organisation which was operating world-wide, but they were nevertheless mistakes of significance which happened under Sir John's own reign and were not generally known outside the company. It was his idea to build a completely new ICI chemical works at a 'green field' site at Wilhelmshaven in North Germany, in parallel with an identical works at Wilton on Teeside, a dual promise which secured the British unions' agreement to the scheme.

According to the unions, millions of pounds were poured into the German site in the expectation that the European market in PVC would boom. In fact the market immediately slumped, millions were lost and the plant was later hived off in a joint deal with the Italians. Ironically Wilhelmshaven was also where Sir John had spent much of his immediate post-war career as an interpreter in the Navy, helping the Russians to ship back a complete German naval dockyard to the Soviet Union. At Wilton, we saw dumped and abandoned pipes originally ordered for the Teeside version of the PVC plant: the machinery was locked and derelict behind a high fence. The whole project seems to have been the victim of bad luck and volatile exchange rates, which ultimately made the product uncompetitive.

Sir John admits that the 'twin strategy' of equal investment at Wilhelmshaven and Wilton was 'a big mistake – because the one we can't load is the Wilton one'. The decision to invest at Wilhelmshaven was, he told us, made after trying to dent the European market in PVC for something like sixteen years: 'People don't seem to understand that trade is like war. Time and time again we'd get a bridgehead and we'd get a little PVC into the European market. The European competitors would just take us out. They'd go in and whatever it cost them, they'd get us out of business.' When ICI actually put a plant in Europe, Sir John claimed, at last the competitors realised that they had lost the bridgehead: 'They could not afford to think that they could throw us back into the sea, and since then we have increased our sales in Europe from literally single figures to over 100,000 tonnes, and a lot of the raw material for that comes from Britain.'

He gave us another example of an attempt to fight into a market in 'the rough tough game of business', as he put it. For years ICI had been trying to supply the European car makers with paint. He could, he told us, understand German reluctance to buy British paint: 'Now if you were a German car manufacturer where the whole of your production line depended on paint, even if you wanted to buy our product because you thought it was better, would you risk the whole of your production through buying paint made in England which has to be shipped across the Channel, with the record that this country has had for interruptions in delivery and so on?' The day ICI started making a dent there, Sir John told us, was when the company set up an alternative source of supply in Germany: 'The technology is in England still, a lot of the paint is supplied from England; but we have an alternative supply base in Germany.'

It is, however, the growth of ICI's investment abroad which is most deplored by his critics, although he claims that it actually safeguards jobs in Britain and that without foreign investment the company could not flourish. The variation in investment at Wilhelmshaven and Wilton, for instance, was, in his view, necessary because the Wilhelmshaven plant was a green field site. The intention to develop two exactly matched units on both sides of the Channel had been stopped 'in mid flight' when it became 'perfectly obvious' that the market estimates had been wrong and that ICI could not possibly support the additional investment.

Sir John is not so ready to agree that the company's more recent foreign investment is dangerous. Union officials, however, are worried that work is moving overseas all the time and have a strong feeling that ICI, by investing abroad, is importing unemployment. When I repeated these views to him, Sir John claimed that the people concerned did not know the facts: 'and since we tell them the facts over and over again, it's a rather sad reflection on their ability to understand the truth of the situation.' He told that nearly sixty per cent of all the investment ICI was putting in in the world was going into the United Kingdom, which had five per cent of the world market but represented twenty-three per cent of ICI sales: 'How, when we are doing that, we can be accused of abandoning the United Kingdom and preferring the rest of the world, just flies in the face of facts,' he commented indignantly.

It was a subject which clearly got under his skin, and when

I said that nevertheless there did seem to be a feeling of resentment that ICI was spending an enormous amount of money by investing abroad, he interrupted to say: 'You can have whatever feelings you like, but the numbers are available there for everyone to look at.' He told us that the company had had 'a fair amount of debate about this' with its shop stewards when the recent purchase of the Beatrice Chemical Company in the United States for $750 million was discussed. 'That's a lot of dollars,' he agreed, 'but what they don't say, but they know, because I've told them, is that the earnings out of that company are paying the interest on the money to buy the company without recourse to anything in England.'

'You see, the whole problem, and what people don't understand . . . well, actually, what people do understand. . . What people don't like – and I have every sympathy with them – is that the markets outside the United Kingdom are growing much faster than the markets inside the United Kingdom,' he explained. He is determined that ICI should keep its present position as one of the world's top five chemical companies, and wants it to be the best company in the world, and moreover the *British* company that is the best chemical company in the world: so, he told us, he has to go where the markets are. 'Look around in the High Street,' he suggested: there we would find proof of his point that if he wants to sell to the electronic industry, he can only sell a disproportionate share of the products that go into tape recorders, videos or radios, if he sells them to Japan.

Selling to Japan, however, presents particular problems: the specifications are different from anywhere else in the world, and the Japanese demand a particularly high level of consistency. Although from Sir John's observation the best British quality is better than the best Japanese, British standards are inconsistent, and the Japanese are absolutely ruthless in discarding a product: 'If you send something which is marginally out on spec. they'll just send it back.' Since Japan is one of the countries where many of the world's leading developments are taking place, and since ICI is supplying industry and must attempt to supply world leaders, Sir John sees the company's growth in Japan as a major aim. In 1985, he welcomed Mr Soichi Saba, the Japanese businessman at the head of the Toshiba Corporation, onto ICI's board as a non-executive director. Toshiba operates in very nearly as many countries as ICI and is, in world terms, almost as big, although Sir John feels that the Japanese perspective on the world is totally different. He said he hoped 'Super Tosh' would be able to help him develop ICI's penetration into the Japanese market and explain 'the quaint old ways of the Japanese'. In 1986, ICI appointed its first American main board director, Tom Wyman, Chairman of CBS, and talked of having become 'a multinational company in the true sense of the word'.

In 1985, Sir John told me, ICI was investing £750 million a year: 'But you can only invest what you earn, and we've only just started earning the sorts of amount we want.' He did not, however, anticipate returning to quite the level of investment of the 1970s because 'the days of that form of investment have gone, because those investments were in very large capital commodity chemicals and the future of the chemical industry is not in that business.'

To the question 'What is the future as you see it of the investment policy of ICI? Is it going to be more and more overseas investment in the Far East and America?' Sir John replied: 'Well, you know I hate to be rude to you as an interviewer, but you are continuing as though I hadn't made a single comment about this. I've already told you several times that this is not our policy and that this is not what we are doing at the moment, and so I find the statement "are you going to do more and more" somewhat offensive. And I'm not being sarky and nasty. I'm just being factual.' He was not, he said, 'ducking the question', but the company did not have a policy as to where it should invest the money: what it did have was a policy 'to make a profit out of the markets wherever the markets are'. There was an overwhelming economic and management case to serve the market from the United Kingdom because 'we've got the people here, we've got the sites, the technical back-up and the research is here. Why should I want to go and build a plant in OshGosh, Iowa, when I've actually got land here and people here who are trained?'

He was insistent that the leaders of ICI were not 'idealogues setting out on some mission to abandon the United Kingdom'. What they were trying to do was to serve markets from the places from which they could be served most economically, and the United Kingdom started with an overwhelming advantage. To underline his point, he said: 'You don't seem to act with any surprise at all when I tell you that we are still investing over sixty per cent of our money in the place with five per cent of the world market which only represents a quarter of our sales.' 'Doesn't that say something to you?' he asked, 'Its absolutely incredible.'

In spite of Sir John's protestations, ICI's Annual Report for 1985 showed continuing growth in Europe, the Americas, Australasia, Japan and the Far East: but it was only in the Americas that the increased turnover was more than matched by an increase in profits. The company's overall turnover had risen, while profits had dropped just below the magic billion mark surpassed in 1984. In the first quarter of 1986 there was a drop in profits of twenty-four per cent, announced in the week that ICI was fined over £6 million for its part in a price-fixing cartel: the other members of the cartel, which between 1977 (before Sir John's reign) and 1983 had met regularly to keep the price of polypropylene artificialy high, were also fined – altogether the European Commission imposed fines of £35 million. ICI was quoted in the press as regretting 'any lapse there may have been from its high ethical standards'. The drop in profits, for the fourth quarter running, was explained by lower oil prices, a lack of demand for bulk fertilisers combined with bad weather, and the exchange rate – in particular the effect of the relationship between the pound and the Deutschmark.

This bore out what Sir John told us, as he had told the House of Lords Select Committee on overseas trade in April 1985, about the problems caused for British industry by fluctuating exchange rates, and their inevitable effect on investment policies: 'The very first question we have to look at when investing a large sum of money in this country is what the added value is and what its export component is.' If the added value was under thirty per cent and the currency fluctuations were more than thirty per cent, he explained, 'you can be the most efficient plant in the world, but you cannot afford to make that product in the United Kingdom and export it. That's not a matter of choice, that's a matter of actual fact.' He is convinced that the effect of exchange rates on exports should be given as much weight in the government's thinking as the effect on the rate of inflation and on interest rates, although he does not claim to have any magic exchange rate formula which the government might be able to use to encourage industry, and admits that there is no evidence that industrialists would be any better at running government than are governments at running industry: 'I think the two skills are quite different. They require different sorts of approach and I think it is presumptious of an industrialist to tell government what to do.' He has said that he has no ambition to enter politics.

Even so, he clearly feels that greater recognition of the exchange rate problem should be made by the government: he 'would settle for an acknowledgement of the problem and an explanation as to why they are trying to do more but can't succeed'. 'It is true,' he told the House of Lords, 'that governments cannot make industrial successes, but they sure as hell can make it a lot more difficult to achieve', and went on to say: 'In all the countries we operate in in the world, this country is the one where the adversarial approach to government has the most extreme affect on industry.'

Nowhere else, he claimed, did industry have to operate under such extreme 'variations in the environment': 'I do not think anywhere else in the world over five years has faced the prospect of nationalisation – it has been rather more frequent recently – and over the next five years has faced the prospect of privatisation, if it had been nationalised.' He found it extraordinary, he told the assembly of eleven lords under the chairmanship of Lord Aldington, 'that it appears to be impossible in this country to have some sort of bi-partisan view of what the industrial role should be and what would constitute a helpful approach to industry as opposed to a hindering one'. It was, he told us, interest rates which affected the exchange rate, and very high exchange rates made it impossible to compete industrially. 'You have to make up your mind whether there is the acceptance of the need for an industrial base – which I believe to be absolutely vital.' Although the necessity of a manufacturing base to provide the wealth to make the country tick over is a belief firmly held by Sir John, he told us, as he had told the Lords, that he did not consider that the acceptance of this was accompanied in Britain by policies and attitudes which would encourage manufacturing. At the top of the list of such policies he would put an acknowledgement of the fact that the exchange rate has at least as much effect on the competitivity of manufacturing as it does on inflation. This would be a start, he said, but the facts argued against it happening.

Sir John was clearly not happy with the record of Margaret Thatcher's government: 'Every government-influenced cost on industry has actually gone up at higher than the rate of inflation over the past few years. My tax bill in the face of a Budget that said it was a Budget for Industry has gone up – not just in absolute terms, but relative to the increase in my profits.' While his profits went up last year by something like sixty-eight per cent, his tax bill more than doubled. If this was meant to be a 'splendidly encouraging way of helping industry', the policy, he suggested, had obviously failed. His local rates had also gone up at a far higher rate than inflation, and his energy costs were 'acknowledged as being uncompetitive'. He was, he complained, frequently accused of moaning when he pointed out that 'If we really want to maintain an industrial base and fight our corner and create wealth, we actually have to start looking at the effect of all the decisions that we wish to take in this country against their effect on manufacturing.' He was not moaning, he claimed, but merely stating the truth: 'We'll do the best we can and we have done the best we can,' he promised, 'and we do remarkably well under the circumstances'. But he told us that he did not see this sort of problem afflicting his competitors in Japan or in Germany.

Whatever the problems of the country and the company, Sir John's personal salary had just risen by sixty-eight per cent. When I asked him why he, as Chairman, had awarded himself this substantial increase, he said, perhaps jokingly, 'If you make that remark again I'll sue you!' He claimed that his vast pay increase had undoubtedly received considerably more attention than the freeze on board salaries throughout his first two years as Chairman, at a time when the pay of everybody else in the company was increased, and explained that shortly after he took over, the non-executive directors who set the company's salary systems said that they felt that a larger part of salaries should be linked to the results of the company: a proposal which he had accepted and which was, he thought, 'a good way to put it'. 'For two years we did not get any pay rise,' he told me, 'the company is now self-evidently more success-ful, and so we got a much larger one than I had expected, but it was done to a formula which had been decided in the first year of my chairmanship. I've produced five different ways in which they could link our payment to the results; it was their decision.' He had therefore, he insisted, had nothing to do with the pay award, which was settled by the board on the advice of the non-executive directors without his being pre-sent.

Whoever made the decision, not everyone would consider a sixty-eight per cent pay rise for the Chairman to be a very good example in an industry where there had been so many redundancies. As Roger Lyons commented: 'It doesn't do a lot for morale where you're sacking people at one end of a company and giving them sixty-eight per cent at the other.' 'Of course, people will always say that,' was Sir John's answer to such criticism, 'and you can take whatever view you do of one man's pay rise and another. . . . you know. The fact of the matter is that if I worked in the States I'd earn four to five times what I earn here'. This is undoubtedly true: we even met one businessman in America while we were making the *Money Makers* series whose income was fifty times the salary received by Sir John Harvey-Jones even when the company is doing well. If it does less well, he stands to lose a third of his current level of pay, and even at his current salary, however 'grossly excessive' some may find it, he still earns nowhere near as much as the highest paid industrialist or television personality in the United Kingdom: 'I am paid less than Terry Wogan, I am paid less than the head of one of the smaller advertising agencies that my company employs. I am not ashamed of my pay, and I believe that my pay should be in the public arena, and I believe that if people want to criticise they should be free to do so. I am perfectly prepared to stand up and take whatever they say, and , doubtless, if our salaries' committee don't like it, they will find ways of reducing my pay. Then it's up to me whether I stay or go.'

His huge pay rise has brought him 'a considerable amount of flak', but money appears to be relatively unimportant as a personal incentive. He does not consider that it buys social esteem or status in Britain, and explains the comparative shortage of successful British entrepeneurs by the general attitude in the country to money, which is he feels far more highly esteemed and eagerly sought after elsewhere, especially in America, where entrepreneurs are looked up to with awe: 'Entrepeneurs, by and large, are motivated by making a lot of money. That is what switches them on and – its a silly thing to say, I suppose – but I think people in England are not quite so switched on by money as people in some other countries.' But he thinks that there is nevertheless an entrepeneurial spirit in Britain, and that the British are extremely good inventors and innovators.

It is putting their innovations into effect that he says the British find more difficult. The chief problems, he claims, are inconsistency in manufacturing, particularly in comparison with the Japanese, and the general attitude in Britain towards industry, which keeps the status of marketing and selling low: 'marketing in this country is seen as a slightly dirty word, and selling is viewed as being a sort of Fuller brush salesman and knocking on doors.' A salesman should, in his view, act as the main fund of information to tell the manufacturer what to make so that he can sell it, rather than merely continuing to sell what others make.

An internal ICI report on recruitment revealed in 1985 that the company had slipped down the list of graduates' employment preferences. It was, Sir John told us, from his point of view not so much a question of quantity as quality. ICI was looking for 250 graduates in 1985: although there would be roughly 100 applications for every job, he said that they might not find the whole 250 that they wanted. This brought him back to the question of the qualities necessary for a career in industry: not only 'toughness and integrity and so on', but also 'humour and drive and the ability to express themselves and a lot of other human qualities' – and, of course, the technical qualifications which ICI still had to look for, because it was, after all, primarily a technical company: 'You couldn't have the company run entirely by ex-sailors like me. At least, you could, but it wouldn't make many chemicals.'

He blames the shortage of suitable applicants partly on government cuts in educational spending, and partly on 'the most appalling way' in which industry portrays itself to young people, who, Sir John feels, as he told the House of Lords, 'wish to follow careers which they see as being of social use and social significance.' He and his fellow industrialists had, he said, 'failed to get the message across . . . that a successful industrial career is a great national and social benefit.' He told us that he often visited universities and talked to undergraduates, but even with his informal and ebullient style it seems that he is no better than others at putting across an attractive image of industry: 'I don't think I switch them on at all. I happen to think I lead a fascinating and privileged life. I don't think they think that. I think they think I lead a life which is full of conflict.' He feels that young people today no longer have the same degree of competitiveness as there was when he was growing up: perhaps, he says, they have learned to value much more 'the ability to work together and harmony, niceness, a harmonious and even tenor or way of doing things as being a highly desirable style of life'.

In the summer of 1985 John Harvey-Jones was knighted in the Queen's Birthday Honours List for Services to Industry. On a rare public appearance for the family, he was accompanied to the investiture at Buckingham Palace by his wife, daughter and granddaughter. When we asked Lady Harvey-Jones, outside the Palace, what she thought was his secret – 'what is it that makes him tick?' – Sir John seemed perhaps ill at ease, but she was suitably non-committal: 'That's a very tricky one to answer – I've got a lot of answers for that.' No, she could not give an individual one – it would be quite impossible. 'Sheer brute force mostly,' he suggested. She was 'terribly happy for him' and 'delighted . . . so proud of him.' His granddaughter told us that he had been given the award 'because he's very clever'.

In April 1986, Sir John gave the annual Dimbleby Lecture on BBC Television. He was more soberly dressed than usual, and gave a muted performance which lacked the ebullience which television audiences had come to expect, but put forward all his usual arguments: industry is a team job – our team against the competitor's team – a team is only as strong as its weakest link; Britain has a switch-off attitude to industry; manufacturers are an endangered species; ICI makes a positive contribution of nearly £2,000 million a year to the balance of payments; identifying bosses with the Tories and the trade unions with Labour has perpetuated a totally outmoded set of adversarial attitudes; we suffer in Britain from short-termism in industrial financing.

His summary of what was needed in British industry was succinct: 'first, exploiting our talent for science and invention, with the emphasis on "exploiting"; second, putting to best effect our ability to do international business; third, getting a fair share or maybe an unfair share of the brightest and best of our young into manufacturing and marketing – and enthusing them; and fourth, learning to be much more skilful at managing industrial change.' 'In America,' he said, 'business is America. In Japan, industrial leaders are the most respected members of society. In Germany, an engineer is referred to in that manner and not plain Mr or Mrs as in the UK.' In Britain, however, 'the best natural leaders have not gone to work in industry, and that is possibly the most important single factor of all.'

Even his critics would agree that Sir John Harvey-Jones is one exception, that he has proved himself to be a natural leader who has gone to work in industry. There are nevertheless some in the company he is said to have rescued who whisper that many of the improvements in ICI's performance after the disasters of 1980 would have come about in any event and were not always attributable to anything he did. Roger Lyons told us that he had noticed that since Sir John's elevation the ties and shirts at head office had become noticeably louder, but thought that when Sir John retired the fashions would once more revert to their usual conservative drabness. 'ICI as an institution can tolerate John Harvey-Jones but they don't necessarily accept his right to change the system in a root and branch manner,' he told us, 'Indeed it would be beyond the capacity of one person to change the system, and the next tier of leadership is already in the system, and the tier after that and the tier after that. One person can't change that much.' When Sir John goes, Mr Lyons says, 'the ICI system is so conservative with a small c, it is so old school tieish that there will be a brain drain'. Mr Lyons forecasts that the executives who succeed him will lack the imagination to 'hold good that part which he's helped to put together and helped to coordinate in ICI'.

Sir John Harvey-Jones will end his chairmanship in 1987. None of the ICI board's three contenders to succeed him seemed likely to have quite his style. While the succession was in doubt, they were known in the company as 'the three aitches': Ronnie Hampel, Tom Hutchison and Denys Henderson; the possibility of an outsider, whose name also happened to begin with 'H', Christopher Hogg of Courtaulds, was also rumoured. Ronnie Hampel, a Cambridge Modern Languages graduate, teetotal, reputed to be strong-willed under an affable exterior, had worked in five of the company's eight divisions, giving him the broadest experience within ICI. Tom Hutchison, with a reputation for being direct and serious, had spent most of his career in ICI's bulk chemical business, and had carried through the cuts and closures in the group's chemical and plastics division. Neither had the board experience of Denys Henderson, at the top of ICI's acquisition team, which he helped to set up in 1984, and of the company's drugs and farm chemicals businesses. Openly ambitious, but more respected than popular, it was Mr Henderson, a Scottish lawyer by training, who was chosen to take over from Sir John Harvey-Jones in 1987.

When the Mr Henderson's appointment as the successor to the chairmanship of ICI was announced, in April 1986, he commented that Sir John would be 'a hard act to follow'.

GIOVANNI AGNELLI OF FIAT

CHAPTER 2

ITALY'S UNCROWNED KING

Giovanni Agnelli, the Chairman of Fiat, and the most powerful private industrialist in Western Europe, has the sort of charisma rare in the modern world of multinationals. Like a cross between a latter day matinée idol and an international diplomat or banker, he is tall, immaculately dressed, with silver hair and an interestingly crumpled face. He wears a larger-than-life wristwatch over the cuff of his shirt, and when making points in conversation, in any of three fluent languages, ticks them off on the fingers of one hand with the energy and conviction of someone who knows what he wants and who is long used to getting it.

His presence exudes effortless authority wherever he goes; his charm, manner, looks and lifestyle have earned him a widespread reputation as 'Italy's uncrowned King', and his industrial empire, inherited from his grandfather, is now so big and influential that no Italian government would dare either to ignore it or to adopt policies which would damage its overall interests.

The headquarters of this empire is in Turin in the Piedmont region of Northern Italy, but its factories and subsidiaries stretch across more than sixty countries, encompassing Fiats, Ferraris and Lancias as well as trucks, trains, trams, tanks and aircraft engines, not to mention a few banks, finance companies, newspapers, a publishing house and a travel agency. Recently, Fiat has started to expand into new high-tech fields such as nuclear power station components and the production of artificial heart valves. More is promised in this direcion.

There is no other private company in Italy which can come anywhere near Fiat in terms of size, wealth and influence abroad. Fiat is still owned and run by the descendants of the man who helped to found it in 1899, an entrepeneurial ex-cavalry officer who was also called Giovanni Agnelli. He was one of a group of men from Piedmont who founded FIAT – Fabbrica Italiana Automobili Torino – with capital of 800,000 Lire. Today, his grandson and namesake is the dominant personality in the company, the man who takes all major decisions and oversees general policy and strategy. To distinguish him from his grandfather, his name is abbreviated by his friends to 'Gianni'; to the rest of Italy he is usually 'l'Avvocato', in deference to his university training in Law. Although he has never used his legal qualification, he has certainly made his mark without it.

'He has a unique quality,' says Arrigo Levi, Editor for five years of the Agnelli-owned national newspaper, *La Stampa*, 'he is charming to both men and women. It's very rare to find anyone who dislikes him. He believes in what he does; he is a unique businessman because he really feels that he has a duty to his company and believes that what is good for Fiat is good for Italy, and what is good for Italy is good for the world.'

This admiration is mirrored throughout the political spectrum. In Rome, Giorgio Napolitano, the foreign affairs spokesman of the Italian Communist Party, agrees that Mr Agnelli's contribution to the modernisation and development of Italian industry is undeniable. Although there are some who say that Mr Agnelli's company is now so big that there is no difference between Fiat and the government, Mr Napolitano considers this view 'too oversimplified': 'Mr Agnelli is independent from political parties in Italy. He never identifies his own position with the position of any political party, but, of course, all governments pay great attention to Mr Agnelli's viewpoint.'

Giovanni Agnelli was born in 1921, the son of Edoardo Agnelli and Princess Virginia Bourbon del Monte di San Faustino. His maternal grandmother, Princess Jane di San Faustino, the daughter of an Italian prince and a Scottish-American Campbell, was considered a great beauty: she was a legendary hostess who entertained in Rome on the grand scale and slept between silk sheets.

The eldest son of a family of seven, Giovanni spent most of

his early years under the influence of an English governess, Miss Parker. In 1935, when he was only fourteen, his father was killed in a seaplane accident. Edoardo Agnelli had been standing on the seaplane's float as it taxied across the water at Genoa – it hit a submerged log, flinging him into the propeller. The widowed Donna Virginia allegedly amused herself after her husband's death by becoming the mistress of, among others, the Italian writer Curzio Malaparte, author of *The Skin* and *The Volga rises in Europe*. Her father-in-law's disapproving attempts to gain custody of her children failed, and eventually a reconciliation was arranged.

Gradually, the family fell under the influence of Giovanni's stern grandfather, Il Senatore, who, in the time-honoured Italian manner of arranging such things, ensured that the Fiat inheritance favoured the male members of the Agnelli line. Giovanni's four sisters were not entrusted with any Fiat position, although one, Susanna, achieved later prominence as a Republican Deputy and then Senator in Rome and author of a best-selling autobiography, *We always Wore Sailor Suits*.

Grandfather Agnelli was keen to groom the young Giovanni for the Fiat succession. He sent him to Detroit in 1939, continuing a tradition of Agnelli family visits to Henry Ford's empire and at the same time keeping a shrewd eye on what the American competition was up to. Two years later, Giovanni joined the Italian Army. He went to the Cavalry School at Pinerolo and later, during the Second World War, served in Russia and North Africa, where he was awarded the Cross for Military Valour. After the Italian Armistice he was a liaison officer with the Americans in the Fourth Allied Army, and when peace came he took a degree in Law at Turin University.

When Il Senatore and Giovanni's mother both died in 1945, the running of the Fiat empire was entrusted to Professor Vittorio Valletta. Giovanni, who was twenty-four, considered himself too young and inexperienced to assume the heavy responsibility which he nevertheless knew was his eventual destiny. Valletta was appointed President of the company in 1946, and was the principle influence on the fortunes of Fiat for the next twenty years. Dictatorial, paternalistic and mercurial –

between 1957 and 1959, 2000 Fiat workers were sacked for daring to contemplate union activities – he was also immensely successful. He established Fiat benefit schemes, housing programmes, nursery schools and holiday camps, and under his leadership the graphs recording factory output, manpower, investment and profits all continued to climb. The total workforce, which in 1899 had barely numbered fifty men, was now approaching 350,000. In Turin, the company town, Fiat was known as 'la Mamma', and it seemed as if there would be no end to constantly increasing production and expansion abroad.

Meanwhile, the young Giovanni had been told by his grandfather to go and enjoy himself while he was still young, and had taken the advice to heart. With a vast personal income, the Fiat heir proceeded to embark on a riotous progression through the most select resorts in Switzerland and the South of France. The newspaper gossip columns chronicled the parties, yachts, fast cars and women, and found them all as irresistible as he did. He had a private aircraft and was close to the Kennedys and Kissinger. As *The Times* put it in an article in October 1985, 'He had a full career in the gossip columns long before he reached the financial pages.'

At five o'clock one morning in 1952, the carefree years came to an abrupt end. While driving his Ferrari at nearly 200 km an hour along the Corniche above Monte Carlo, Giovanni Agnelli collided with a stationary meat truck. Miraculously, he survived, but his leg was broken in six places and he had to spend three months in hospital. The crash left him with a pronounced limp and meant that he had to give up riding, although not driving fast cars: Ferraris maintain their allure. The accident changed his life in other ways. Within a year, and still hobbling on sticks, he married a Neapolitan Princess, Marella Caracciolo di Castagneto, a former Vogue photographer, and became active as Fiat's Vice-president (a post he had held since 1945). In 1966 he became Chairman.

We first met Mr Agnelli on the roof-top test track of Fiat's derelict Lingotto car factory in the middle of Turin. He was there to indulge in a few hair-raising circuits in his favourite vehicle – a souped-up Fiat saloon – while his bodyguards, who are said to need special training in high-speed driving and who normally have to try to keep up with him through the Italian traffic, had a chance to relax. Mr Agnelli's accident does not seem to have curbed his lust for speed. Throughout a demonstration of rallying skill, he managed to control the car in spite of the fact that because of his injured leg, one foot is incapable of pressing any of the pedals.

I asked him what he felt about the security risks he faced as the biggest symbol of Italian capitalism. 'The worst years in terrorism in Italy have passed,' he said, 'They were the late seventies and early eighties and the number of people, judges, political people, shot at in cars, and killed and knee-capped were many.' This number was now going down, he told us, but he still believed that there was a certain amount of international terrorism in Europe, and that a few people were still the targets of terrorists who would certainly take any chance to shoot, and might succeed. He nevertheless felt able to drive around quite easily in Italy, and claimed that there were few people who recognised him, although his fame makes this seem unlikely – in one year, 1975, his photograph adorned the front page of eleven national magazines.

'So, how is security handled?' he asked, 'Mainly by the car following you, which can be of some help if they want to kidnap you and can be of help in trying to shoot if something happens.' He did not, he told us, like using armoured cars, although these were absolutely bullet-proof 'so long as you avoid being shot at in the front or the side.' The extra weight of an armoured car ruined his pleasure in driving: 'I think an armoured car kills a car. It's like adding four or five passengers to it permanently. The acceleration goes down, the brakes go down.' At first, he admitted, he had found having security people around 'very disturbing and really rather shaming' – but 'one gets used to it' and now he claims that he personally never thinks about it.

In spite of the security problems, he has stayed in Italy when he could have gone to live somewhere else, and could perhaps even have made very much more money by doing so. Making more money and living without the need for security were, however, not sufficient incentives for leaving his country: 'My place is here, so is my job, and my family is always looked after here.' Leaving Italy was 'totally out of the question, it's never given a second thought'. Even when he is travelling – he makes, for instance, at least half a dozen trips a year to the United States – he is never away for more than a week at a time. What keeps him in Italy, he told us, is that 'This company was started by my grandfather in the other century. It's a small part but it's a successful part of Italy and the economy. It has always been run by my family and I have enjoyed running it all my life.'

Mr Agnelli invited us to join him in his helicopter, which was airborne from the factory car park in moments, and gave us an aerial guided tour of his industrial kingdom and favourite city. From the air we could see the curving River Po with the elegant squares and elaborate buildings of central Turin laid out on either side. We flew low over the military part of the town and the royal palace – 'We practically had the Crown Prince of Italy living here until 1932 or 33'. Then our guide ordered the pilot to fly us over the giant Mirafiori complex on the outskirts of Turin. All we could see below were rows of workshops and car parks.

'This automobile factory was built in 1940 and it was, in a way, the biggest unit one could ever have for cars,' he told us. 'We would never do a thing like that again because today we would never want to have units of more than 5000 to 6000 workers. Here we've had up to 50,000 to 60,000. It's a terribly difficult way of working. It's inconvenient for the workmen to come here and there are difficult labour relations; it's uncontrollable in the event of any terrorist trouble.' His visits to the factories are now infrequent, although he said that he used to visit them more often while they were being built and immediately following their construction: 'Now, if there is a special reason I go and see them, but I'm not familiar with the day-to-day operation or with the life that goes on in them.' The rarity of his visits to the factories is not, he explained, a deliberate choice, but is inevitable as he has 'other work, other things to do': 'When you are the centrehold, you have got a lot of things to do which are maybe less attractive than factory life – but they become very important.' Planning, taxes, financing, relations with the stockholders, the stock market, all have to take priority.

When we had been in the air for about twenty minutes, the helicopter ducked under a layer of low cloud as the pilot found a valley leading towards the foothills of the Italian Alps. Suddenly we came upon a church and mansion set in the greenest of parkland at Villar Perosa. The house was bought by Mr Agnelli's great-great-grandfather, we were told, as a shooting lodge after he had tired of being in Russia with Napoleon. The founder of Fiat was born there and the younger Giovanni lived there in the 1950s, although nowadays he lives in town and only has time to come occasionally for lunch or for official functions at the church, which was currently being restored: he would, he told us, attend the first mass when the restoration was finished. From 1945 until 1980, he was also Mayor of the village of Villar Perosa, a position he inherited along with the family business from his grandfather, who had held it from 1895.

When the helicopter had landed on the pad below the main lawns, we walked towards the house. In the distance, guard dogs bayed from their kennels; the church clock chimed and there was no sound of traffic, only a background of birdsong. Someone had arranged a group of elegant chairs on an immaculate lawn, and there we continued our conversation.

When did Mr Agnelli first realise that he would one day have to take over Fiat, I asked him. 'I knew that sooner or later I would have to do it,' he said, 'I was in the Army for quite a while and then I had a good time for quite a few years, but I knew the moment would come when I would have to take it over so I always had my mind on it; I really took it over in the first person when I was forty.' By then, of course, he had a reputation for being something of a playboy: 'Those were the happy, good days, yes – but time passes.' Even during his playboy years, he had known that he would end up by having to be responsible for the family's business empire: 'That was why I was having it as good as possible for the short time I could.' It was said at the time that he had an income of a million pounds a year, but he was vague about the amount: 'It's so difficult to say because in the post-war days everything was so dangerous. You never knew how Italy would turn out. Czechoslovakia was falling one day; we had a General Election; the Communists might have taken over.' All this apparently made it very difficult to calculate an income. 'Then there were the years when the profits were colossal; some people burned them away, others invested in their companies; we invested more than we spent. If not we would not be here now.'

The prospect of taking over the responsibility had not seemed awe-inspiring to him because, like the heir to a throne, he knew it was inevitable: 'I was born feeling it that way . . . I wouldn't say that I was looking forward to doing it very soon because I had a very very good man, Professor Valletta, who was running the company and it was all his life.' Giovanni appreciated Professor Valletta's skills all the more because he could enjoy having more time to himself, but was 'very close to him and very fond of him, and he was very fond of me'. But he told us that he thought he should probably have taken over one or two years earlier than he did – Valletta carried on until he was in his eighties: 'The last two years were not as brilliant as the rest had been. So I should have taken over one or two years before.'

To a question about what he most enjoyed about running Fiat, he replied without hesitation: 'I think that what one enjoys is the success – it's the only real answer.' There have inevitably been occasional failures as well as successes, and Mr Agnelli admitted that one of his biggest mistakes was in the mid-1960s when, because he felt that the European motor car industry was too divided and sectorised he had tried to work out a merger with Citroen. Technically and commercially this made sense, he told us, and when the two companies actually got together for two or three years he thought that it would be possible: 'But, obviously, I misjudged how strong nationalistic feelings at that moment still were in a country like Italy, or France, or maybe in many other countries; so we had to come to a separation. We didn't even get to scramble the eggs.' He still felt that the idea and the direction, and the general strategy, were absolutely correct, but realised that the attempt to put it into effect had been premature. This was a mistake which was still being made, he told us: 'Everything that goes on in Europe today is the same thing. Everybody's trying to press things that people are not yet ready to accept.'

Although Giovanni Agnelli's four sisters still have no active role in the family business empire, his brother Umberto has already been named as his successor. Umberto, who is fifteen years younger, is Fiat's Vice-president and has dabbled in politics as a Democrat senator. His decision to stand as a Democrat in the 1975 elections came as something as a surprise to the family, as there was at the time a suggestion first that a new centre-left party might be formed with Giovanni Agnelli as its leader, and then that Giovanni would stand as a Republican. In fact, Giovanni has never entered the political arena. His sister Susanna, a Republican Senator, has said that he would find the life of a deputy boring, and that it would not satisy his constant restlessness, an opinion echoed by others who know him.

Giovanni is convinced that it is in Fiat's interests to have a firm line of family succession. Umberto 'has lived into the company and knows it very very well,' he told us, 'I believe he'd be able to pick good management for it and I hope there would be a continuity. I can't look any further than that.' He anticipates that the company will still be controlled in the indefinite future by the family, which, although he has only one son and one daughter himself, is vast: when Fiat's PR team drew up a family tree a few years ago, they found that he had no fewer than seventy-eight cousins. In his opinion the continuity is good for the company, or at least has always proved itself to be so in the past: 'I think for the management to rely on a stability of appointment in somebody who has proved to know the problems of the company has been an advantage for it.' He does not see 'how the judgement of someone who has been trained and brought up in it should be worse than any – God forbid – politically appointed manager when they take over from anybody else.'

It may seem like a form of inherited benevolent nepotism, but he told us that this must, almost automatically, be to the advantage of all concerned with the company since 'the purpose we have is only the future of the company, the success of the growth of the company. We don't have any other.' To him, it is obvious that Agnelli interests are exactly the same as the interests of the company, and that the same identification of interests could not be possible in a state enterprise: 'First, you have managers appointed politically and politically things change – one party comes to power and then another party comes to power – they've got political loyalties. They don't choose management out of the best quality, they choose it out of friendship or other purposes.' Not that it was impossible for a state industry to have very good managers – 'It can happen that they have good and bad, and then they can be appointed for special reasons. We've seen it happen again and again.'

Fiat has always had one state-owned competitor – Alfa Romeo. Giovanni Agnelli says that he has known both their figures and his figures for half a century. He gets on very well with Alfa Romeo, he told us, but added: 'I am sorry as a taxpayer, because we all contribute to their losses regularly year after year.' Alfa Romeo started life in 1910 as the Anonima Lombarda Fabbrica Automobili. The second part of its name came from a mining engineer, Nicola Romeo, who in 1916 was busily making pumps for the Italian Army; he was so successful that he had to look for new investments and more factory space. Joining forces with Giuseppe Merosi, an ex-building surveyor and bicycle manufacturer, he adopted the cross and serpent badge of Milan as the new company crest, and together they started the world-famous line of high-performance sports and racing cars.

Alfa Romeo flourished for some time with a series of brilliant successes on the international racing circuit. In the thirties, however, their cars became too specialised; production numbers started to fall and eventually the company was only saved from bankruptcy by being taken over by a government which wanted it to earn prestige for the state by building aero engines, winning races and turning out a few exotic cars. In the Second World War the factories in Milan were almost all destroyed by Allied bombing, but in the post-war years the company was recreated and under a brilliant engineer, Dr Satta Puliga, embarked on the mass production of saloon cars.

Today, its headquarters on the outskirts of Milan is a glittering example of modern design and give no hint of the production problems the company has faced in its subsidiary factories, particularly those near Naples. The President of Alfa Romeo, Ettore Massacesi, does not deny that the company has faced severe difficulties, but is obviously peeved by the criticisms of his firm by Fiat's main spokesman. He told us that the reasons for his company's recent problems were more complex than Mr Agnelli had suggested. True, Alfa Romeo had made losses for a number of years, but performance was now definitely improving and any company of its size and speciality would have faced similar difficulties, whether it had been state or privately owned. State ownership, he said, was not always a recipe for financial disaster: he cited an example of a loss-making Fiat plant which was sold to the government and was now making a profit.

Fiat's great strength, Mr Massacesi told us, is its unique share of the home market – seventy per cent of the production is sold in Italy. It is, he says, Fiat's monopoly of the Italian market, not sales to the rest of Europe or America, which has made Mr Agnelli's company so powerful and successful. But Fiat, which employs over 200,000 workmen and whose sales are less than half of those of the state-owned industries, Alfa Romeo included, makes money while the others lose it: 'That's the difference,' Mr Agnelli told us, 'That just gives us more flexibility towards the people.'

Giovanni Agnelli does not agree with those who say that Fiat is so big and so influential that it is almost indistiguishable from the Italian government. Surely the state-owned industries have more influence, he suggests: 'Their managers are appointed by the government; they press, they petulate [sic], they ask for money, they insist. When I need money I have to go to the market for it and it's very very difficult. But when they need money they go to the government and it's quite different.'

Fiat has never had any kind of state assistance, other than that available to everyone through, for instance, support for research or help towards redundancy payments: 'I'll tell you just why we have never had any state support,' Mr Agnelli explained, 'If I ever had it Fiat would lose its freedom, and freedom is our main aim.' He is determined that Fiat will never fall into the hands of the state, but nevertheless considers his most difficult task as company Chairman to be judging the relationship with the Italian government, as well as the Italian public, and seeing that the company is more popular than the rest of industry in the country: 'We have to be on the best possible terms with the government, but we do not have and we have never had influence on the government.' Fiat today represents about four per cent of Italy's GNP, he told us, and he thinks it should be respected for that. As it contributes about 2.5 million dollars net to the Italian economy, and pays about a billion dollars a year in taxes, he considers its contribution to the community big, although he estimates its influence on the government as very small.

As head of Fiat, he told us that he no longer runs the day-to-day operation, although he had 'looked into that in the past', but claimed that nothing of major importance happened without his approval: 'and if there is my disapproval it doesn't happen.' He said that all the Directors were named 'under my judgement' and that no major financial transaction was engaged in without his judgement as a shareholder. His relationship with top management has, he told us, always been excellent: 'I hardly see how we could have lived without each other.'

Fiat today is a holding company of fifteen different industries. Mr Agnelli represents his family holding, which has thirty-two per cent of the voting shares: 'It's one third of 100,000 shareholders. It's not so extraordinary,' he told us. He does not consider that the economic power in the hands of one family is enormous. Taking a country like Switzerland or Holland and considering the weight that Shell, Nestle or Unilever carry in those countries, he considers this to be infinitely bigger than the weight that Fiat carries in Italy, and claims that the most significant thing about Fiat in Italy is not its size, but its efficiency.

The holding company appoints the managers of the fifteen different activities, including the motor car industry with sales of $10 billion a year, tractors with sales of $3 billion, tool machines, components, racing engines and so on. 'We have the summing up of the strategy of all these companies,' he told us, 'and the appointment of the management and their financial policy, giving priorities to support – will we increase our capital? Will we go into finance first? And to what extent? I would say that that is a main judgement.' In a company with over 200,000 employees there are inevitably huge problems: 'There are problems of credit with the banks, of relations with the shareholders, of relations with government, and relations with your competitors. I would say there are more problems than you have time for.'

One of the most difficult things about running the company is, he told us, getting the right people, getting on well with the right people and having the best people to run the company. There is, however, no room for a battle of wills at the top, as was demonstrated when in 1976 Carlo De Benedetti, now Chairman of Olivetti and, after Agnelli, Italy's most prominent businessman, became Managing Director of Fiat. After a hundred days, he left: Mr Agnelli later said that although Mr De Benedetti was 'very good', he was 'totally inappropriate for Fiat because he wanted to be boss in our home'. Mr De Benedetti put it slightly differently: 'If you are a king like Mr Agnelli, you're for the monarchy. If you're not, you're a republican. I am a republican and he is a king.'

Even as a king with a recognised line of succession, Mr Agnelli sees differences between his reign and that of his grandfather. He has described Giovanni Agnelli the First as 'a capitalist entrepreneur', 'an industrialist . . . a real self-made man', 'the "padrone" who took the risks and made the decisions'. Il Senatore's basic aim was, according to his grandson, not so much profit as progress, but he had more enthusiasm, amounting to a passion, for technical than for social progress. At the same time, he insisted on selecting his own staff and would never have trusted a personnel department to do this for him, preferring to discover the right men by moving around his factories and then to give huge responsibilities to those he trusted. 'My grandfather was the typical old-fashioned master, who moved freely within his domains, and when he saw talent, when he met men of quality, he took a risk and took them with him,' Mr Agnelli told Arrigo Levi in a series of interviews published in 1983, 'Quite a different concept from the one prevailing today.'

As Chairman of the Agnelli family-owned holding company, IFI (Istituto Finanziario Industriale), and its international subsidiary (IFI International), Giovanni Agnelli may not wield quite the same absolute power as did his grandfather, but he nevertheless controls a formidable list of his family's assets. These encompass insurance, financial services, unit trusts, cement, department stores, hotels (three per cent of Club Mediteranée), food and drink (fifty per cent of Cinzano), newspapers (*La Stampa*), a publishing house (Fabbri-Bompiani-Etas), and even the soccer team Juventus. He and his brother Umberto share a fanatical interest in football and rarely miss watching their team, which has always been owned by the family.

The vast Agnelli empire was not acquired overnight. The roots of its growth lie in the twenties and thirties when Grandfather Agnelli halved production costs, launched a new series of cheap small cars, and moved from the Lingotto factory to the new works of Mirafiori north west of Turin, where the site had a million square metres, 300,000 of them under cover, and 22,000 employees worked on shifts. Prosperity was achieved by a combination of good management and planning, luck, and hard work. It also depended on smooth relations with government: Fiat had arms contracts from the Fascists and Mussolini himself visited the factory in Turin.

Judging from some of the photographs in Fiat's archives, many workers welcomed him enthusiastically: they can be seen giving the Fascist salute. Grandfather Agnelli was dressed for the occasion in Fascist uniform. When we asked his grandson about the relationship between Fiat and Mussolini, he told us that between 1924 and the end of the War Italian industry was run in a corporate regime, which looked on industry as a tool of consumption inside and a tool of military ambitions outside. Yes, Fiat was making arms, but only in a very small way, and it was making very good aeroplanes. In 1938 there were Fiat planes in the Spanish Civil War, and in 1935–36 the fastest aircraft in the world was, he told us, a Fiat, which he said surely proved that at that stage in aviation technology Fiat was in the lead.

What about the relationship between Fiat and Mussolini? Fiat was a big industry in a very independent town (Turin), and 'very reserved'. At the time it had, he thought, about 30,000 workmen: 'They were always a certain worry to Mussolini because when he saw all these workmen he knew that it was not a Fascist unit and he always used to say that Fiat workers were like figs – black outside but red inside.'

The communists in Italy see this episode in a different light. Mr Napolitano is convinced that there was some compromise and co-operation between the Fascists and industry. 'You cannot imagine the life and growth of Fiat between the early twenties and the end of the Second World War without such co-operation,' he told us, 'It probably was unavoidable, but nevertheless there was this co-operation.' When I put it to him that Mr Agnelli had said that although there might have been superficial co-operation, Fiat had been black on the outside and red on the inside, Mr Napolitano replied with a twinkle: 'I think that's probably true as regards workers. But we were speaking of the grandfather of Mr Agnelli – I don't think he was red inside.'

Red or not, Fiat continued to grow. After the war, Professor Valletta ordered a vast restructuring programme and new production was developed in all sectors. In 1955, the new Fiat 600 model was launched, the Mirafiori factory was enlarged and production reached 1000 cars a day. In 1963, the Group produced 956,000 cars and trucks and 38,000 tractors. Two years later, Fiat was producing more than a million vehicles a year, and had signed an agreement with the Russians to help build and run the Togliattigrad car factory in the Soviet Union with an annual production capacity of 600,000 vehicles. By this time the Group had other joint deals with Argentina, Spain, Turkey, Poland, Yugoslavia and Brazil.

In the 1950s and '60s, thousands of workers moved from the impoverished southern parts of Italy to find work in the plains of the North. Many came to Turin, swelling the ranks of Fiat and surrounding the factory suburbs in rows of state-owned apartment blocks. This internal migration was often cited as one cause of Italy's growing social and economic problems. Mr Agnelli was blamed by the Left for taking advantage of a pool of cheap labour, but doing nothing to solve the housing problems of newly arrived immigrants. He shrugged off such accusations by observing that the first wave of immigration anywhere was always traumatic, and that if Fiat had built car factories in the South, the company would probably have gone bankrupt; at least Turin was profiting by the continuing expansion in the North and he was convinced that its prosperity would inevitably eventually benefit everyone.

Many businessmen and politicians in Italy became suspicious of Mr Agnelli in the mid-seventies for rather different reasons. As President of Confindustria, an association of Italian industrialists and manufacturers similar to Britain's CBI, he had struck a deal in 1975 with Luciano Lama, Italy's most powerful union leader and head of the Communist-dominated CGIL (General Federation of Labour). The agreement laid down wage rises linked to cost of living increases for workers which, in some cases, were more than a hundred per cent. Many Italians subsequently blamed the Lama-Agnelli agreement for the staggering inflation which followed.

At the time Mr Agnelli countered such criticism by claiming that it was better that the unions should get what they wanted in the beginning than that everyone should face a long period of conflict which might very well end with the same result. Instead he blamed politicians for high public expenditure and inefficient administration. He did not expand in public, however, on another claim his critics had made: that the lira had been devalued as a direct result of the agreement and that this allowed Fiat to make extra profits from boosted foreign sales.

Mr Arrigo Levi, the former Editor of La Stampa, told us that the indexation agreement, by which a cost of living increase automatically increased wages, had turned out to be a very bad one, but that whatever the Left-wing economists said this was not entirely Agnelli's fault: 'I would say that everything in Italy at that time turned in favour of inflation. Everybody seemed to think that having inflation and development was better than having no inflation and no development. We needed development so badly. The Agnelli agreement did add to that inflation, although at the time it was considered to be the sort of agreement which would bind national peace. Instead it cost a lot of money, it did not bind national peace and actually led to a succeeding deterioration of relations on an unimaginable scale. Some of the big industries like Fiat itself had become ungovernable. Then Agnelli, although guilty of weakness before, found enough strength to say "Basta" – "that's enough".'

In the 1970s, Fiat, like every other industry in Europe, was desperately trying to adjust to the effects of the oil crisis and world recession. Demand had slumped and there were growing problems of over-capacity and over-manning. At the same time the Group had also become the biggest symbol of Italian capitalism and therefore a target for the emerging Red Brigades. In Turin, bombs were planted in Fiat's factories. In separate attacks four Fiat workers were killed and twenty-seven injured; 200,000 cars were lost through sabotage. In 1979, when Agnelli effectively said 'Basta', Fiat sacked sixty-one leftist militants. The company was restructured, new tough managers were appointed, like Cesare Romiti, formerly the head of Alitalia, and, in the face of losses of more than £100 million, it was announced that one in ten workers would be made redundant.

The unions retaliated with a strike which shut down Fiat for more than a month. The FLM (Federazione Lavoratori Metalmeccanici – the Metal Workers' Union) ordered a walk-out, and the Communist leadership urged the workers to take over their factories. The crisis lasted for thirty-five days and ended only when the moderates decided to take matters into their own hands. In an extraordinary act of cinema, 40,000 of the rank and file marched through the middle of Turin in a now famous counter-demonstration to show their exasperation with the leadership and with having to exist for so long without wages. Today in Turin the protest is still known as 'the march of the 40,000'. The unions stood up to the Red Brigades too and eventually accepted 23,000 redundancies. It is now generally agreed that the turning point of Fiat's fortunes was the sacking of the militants.

'We had to fire sixty-one workmen and, naturally, the trade unions protected them immediately,' Mr Agnelli told us,

'We had to go to court and of these sixty-one, I think, forty-five were found to have been real terrorists – people who had shot at or who were ready to shoot at people, or who were organising terrorism. The fact is that in those days we really were under the threat of these left-wingers. The work was low; there was dope sold in the factories; the respect for discipline was nil – I mean things had to get very very bad before you could hit at them and they started getting better.'

He had not so much allowed the situation to exist, he told us, as been a victim of the political situation in the country in 1969 and 1970, which he compared with 1968 in France. The seventies were, as he put it, 'a permanent loss': of discipline generally, of control of the government over the people and of discipline inside the factories. He claimed that the general 'disregard and disrespect' had had a certain amount of support from the mass media: 'We got this unlucky position of a very big Communist party and a situation where one might have lost completely. It really was a breaking point.' Fiat's internal problems were not, he insisted, the fault of the company's management, but rather of a very fast growing industrial civilisation: 'We had a lot of immigration in Turin, of new workmen coming in, people who had come from the South and had come into contact with an industrial civilisation which did not easily tolerate them.' It was admittedly the very fast industrial growth which had resulted in an excessive accumulation of people in the city: if he could go back, Mr Agnelli told us with the benefit of hindsight, he would not have had so many people coming to Turin, and would have started to decentralise the factories earlier.

In 1985, Fiat had reduced its workforce by almost 30,000 people, approximately ten per cent of its total employees. When I asked him why, Mr Agnelli gave much the same explanation as that given by Sir John Harvey-Jones to questions about sackings in ICI: no industry can afford to employ more people than are strictly necessary for competitive productivity. The need to reduce manpower was, in Fiat's case, linked to what Mr Agnelli termed 'a moment when technology bites in new forms': it was then not that one wanted to sack people, but that one could not afford to have more people than necessary when technology imposed itself for production reasons. 'I cannot allow employment to be in the way of new technology and not use it,' he said, 'Otherwise my competitors will do it and everybody's job will be endangered.' Although Fiat had sacked 13,000 out of 245,000 employees in one year, he pointed out that only four or five per cent had lost their jobs with the company: 'and with the leaps and bounds in technology these days, a five or six per cent personnel reduction is not a very big figure.' He expected similar reductions in personnel in motor car industries throughout the world. 'The only real way of creating employment is creating something competitive and efficient,' he told us, 'if you have something inefficient, you kill employment everywhere.'

He turned the suggestion that he had himself contributed towards the country's unemployment figures aside: 'I think I am considered as having made the jobs of the people in Fiat much stronger and more safe than they were before. So when you have 230,000 people working for you, and their jobs are strong and safe, I think it's an achievement. If I had 300,000 it would endanger the jobs of everybody. I would not be doing my job correctly.'

That might not be the way some of the people who had been sacked would see it, I suggested. 'Sacking' was a word he did not like, he said, preferring to call it 'mobility of labour': 'This really means that people have to be ready to prepare for and accept new jobs in different places and probably at different wages.' In Italy, as in most of Europe, about two million people, ten per cent of the workforce, were unemployed: in Europe as a whole there were over twenty million people out of work. At the same time, Mr Agnelli said that we must consider that in Italy there had been one and a half million immigrants, which was a new phenomenon in the country: 'It's not like in France or in your country. We've got three million people in what are called black-market or moon-lighting jobs. So if you put two million officially unemployed, with over three million moon-lighting jobs, one and a half million immigrants and a certain mobility and deregulation, one could probably have used those two millions better than they have been in the past . . . twenty million unemployed in Europe is a big mass of potential talent.'

He sees the biggest employment problem in Italy, as elsewhere, to be among the young, with nearly a third of those between eighteen and twenty out of work: 'That is very troubling because these people are hardly remunerated at all since they have never had a first job.' But he does not consider the unemployment of the 1980s to be as serious as that of the 1930s, because of the various 'shock absorbers' which have been built by different societies in different countries and which make current unemployment less likely to lead to revolution than between 1929 and 1932.

In the mid-1970s the effects of the oil crisis left Fiat with serious financial problems as well as those of internal security and labour relations. Mr Agnelli's solution was to seek help from the Arabs. In a secret deal worth £250 million, he persuaded the Libyans to take a ten per cent holding in Fiat, later increased to fourteen per cent, with two representatives on the fifteen-strong main Fiat board. The deal was characteristic of the Agnelli approach – skilful, novel and imaginative; it was negotiated secretly in Milan and took his fellow country-men completely by surprise. In some quarters there were inevitably questions about its wisdom. *La Stampa*, Mr Agnelli's own national newspaper, was the first to react. Mr Arrigo Levi, then the Editor, was a Jew and a Zionist who felt strongly about a Fiat link with Colonel Gaddafi and said so in an editorial. It was, Mr Levi told me, the only article he had ever written which the owner of *La Stampa* had demanded to see before it was published. Mr Levi claimed that he had been against the deal primarily because he thought that it would compromise the independence of Fiat: 'The danger was in being linked to a man who was considered world-wide as a dangerous character and who was organising disruptions and acts of terrorism everywhere.' He also told us that in 1983 Libya had asked for his dismissal from *La Stampa* because he was a Jew, had written a critical article about Colonel Gaddafi and had fought in the 1948 Arab/Israeli war. Apparently Colonel Gaddafi had even boycotted Fiat for a time as a result of the article, but Mr Agnelli stood by his Editor and the problem, it seems, eventually went away. 'Obviously, between Mr Gaddafi and myself there was, to some extent, an open account,' Mr Levi said. 'We will see who wins in the end.'

Why, I asked Mr Agnelli, did he accept money from Libya. 'We did not accept money,' he said, 'We had Libyans coming in as shareholders. This was in a moment of difficulty in 1976 and at that moment, I remember, Kuwait went into Daimler Benz, Iran went into Krupp and the Libyans were looking for an investment which would even be a status symbol in some European countries.' His way of explaining that Fiat did not take money from the Arab Libyan Bank was not exactly convincing to a layman: 'We increased capital and the Arab Libyan Bank put money into Fiat, coming in on very good conditions for Fiat at that moment because money was very difficult and I think they were a real help.' He had, he told us, found the Directors appointed by the Libyans to the Fiat board – one the Governor of the Central Bank, the other the Minister of Heavy Trade – to be 'excellent directors and professionally, I always say, as good as a Swiss bank can be.' The effect on Fiat of having the controversial Libyan money was 'just having new cash coming in – that's all.'

Although he could hardly have foreseen it at the time, the Libyan connection was later to become something of an embarrassment. When President Reagan started accusing Gaddafi of orchestrating terrorism, and in April 1986 ordered a bombing raid on Tripoli, Fiat's board began to fear that their business in the United States might suffer because of strong anti-Libyan feeling. The Agnelli family wanted to buy the Libyans out, but Gaddafi was not interested as the Fiat investment was earning so much for Libya. In Washington, there was a strong feeling against giving a contract worth nearly $8 million for 178 bulldozers to Fiat-Allis, even though their bid was better than American alternatives, because it might be construed as giving financial sustenance to Libya's support of international terrorism.

Earlier in 1986, Fiat had refuted suggestions that as a member of the Sikorsky consortium's American bid for West-land helicopters it might allow the Libyans access to American technology. When the political scandal about the sale of Westland helicopters broke in Britain, Mr Agnelli's skill in international dealings was well illustrated. He had for some time been looking for an opportunity to diversify from cars and trucks into newer businesses like aerospace, and managed to ensure that Fiat's interests were somehow represented on both sides in the rival bids for Westland. How he manoeuvred himself into a position where he could not lose is still not clear. In *Not With Honour – the Inside Story of the Westland Scandal*, Magnus Linklater and David Leigh claim that there were 'subterranean plans' for Fiat to take over Agusta, the Italian helicopter firm who were to be part of the European bid for Westland. But Fiat was dealing at the same time with Sikorsky, 'one of the murkiest areas of the Westland affair', according to the authors. Fiat's willingness to 'pay through the nose for the arrangement . . . is something which has never been fully explained', they maintain.

When the original deal with Libya had been made, however, Mr Agnelli had not expected the political situation to have any adverse financial effect on his business interests. He dismissed the suggestion that by accepting Libyan money, he was in effect allowing the Russians to get into a NATO country through the back door: 'It was a financial investment at a moment when we needed money. There's no influence of any kind. They have never asked us anything and I must say they have never given us any advantages either.' If he had hoped that his company might, as a result of the deal, find an entry into some particular market in Africa, that had never happened either, but he did not enlighten us as to whether this had in fact ever been the intention. One way or another there had, he told us, never been anything in the deal except a financial investment which had worked to everyone's advantage: 'They happen to have made a very good investment because the last few years in Fiat have been very successful, but at the moment when they came in they were very brave, and they came in on very expensive terms.'

Fiat was able to use the Libyans' money to invest in automation and introduce a completely new series of car designs. At the end of the 1970s the reputation of Fiat cars abroad was hardly flattering. Because of all the troubles at the factories in Turin, their products had become notorious for rust and unreliability, and the company desperately needed a new image. By the end of 1980 it had found one. The corner was turned when the 40,000 shop-floor workers and middle management came onto the streets of Turin for their famous silent march. The protest signalled the end of the union resistance to Fiat's redundancy plans and the end of more than a decade of ever increasing union influence. At the same time a new period of more assertive management coincided with an investment programme – 5400 billion Lire over five years – which Fiat hoped would ensure the success of their new 'Tipo Uno' and leave the competition far behind. By 1983 productivity had increased by twenty per cent, turnover by eleven per cent, and car profits were more than £36 million. These advances were comparatively modest but the trend continued.

The British car industry was faring rather differently while Fiat expanded, and I asked Mr Agnelli for his opinion on the problems which have beset British Leyland. 'I remember it in the past,' he said, 'It was a luxury car industry because it had something like thirty-five different factories and they started getting together and assembling. Then I remember when you had one unit of automobiles in England – you convinced Lord Stokes, who ran Leyland, to put it together . . . I think he felt he was very patriotic taking the whole thing over, and he damaged his truck business which was excellent and very well run.' It became, according to Mr Agnelli, a 'very-difficult-to-integrate car industry'.

He did not, he told me, feel that the British had made a fundamental mistake in trying to integrate: 'I think they should have integrated but that is very very difficult. If you start a new motor car industry from scratch like the Japanese, then its very easy, but if you have a long history, with lots of different motor car factories, with all the love there was for the motor car in England and all the differentiation of the designs, the styles, colours, formulas, ways of building cars and you have to put them together – it's very difficult. It's easier to kill them and start again than to put them all together.'

There were, he said, now two British car industries: one was that of the Americans in England – General Motors and Ford, which had always done well or fairly well – and the other, 'the real English', was the successor to British Leyland. The British decision to start working with the Japanese was, in his opinion, very risky because they came from a different civilisation and had a different way of thinking and working. 'I would not want them to think that through Great Britain they could use a Trojan Horse to come into the Common Market and then assemble their own constructions and sell them to the English end,' he told me, 'I've always been – I don't say suspicious of the Japanese – but they are very very strong competitors and one has to be very careful.'

Although he was not, he insisted emphatically, in any way jealous of what the British had been able to arrange, and was not a protectionist, he thought that on the whole the European industry should be careful about allowing other 'Trojan Horses' in. The Americans had been in Europe for so long – Ford, since before the 1914 War, and General Motors had moved in between the wars – that by now they could be considered European: they behaved and thought like Europeans, they had European management and knew the European problems. But he thought that there would be a certain amount of danger if the Japanese came in: 'They would be new; at home their costs have been so low that they would create a protectionist feeling and I don't think that's good in any way for Europe.'

In early 1985, Fiat held discussions with Ford of Europe about a possible merger. The feasibility studies were completed for a whole range of options in what promised to be the biggest ever shake-up in the European motor industry. In theory the proposed merger would have given a Fiat/Ford group a quarter of the market, but when news that discussions were being held was leaked to the media, the talks soon ran into difficulty and were eventually postponed. Neither side wanted to concede control to the other.

Our interview with Agnelli took place before this stage had been reached, and I asked Mr Agnelli what he thought the implications would be for the British car industry if the proposed Fiat/Ford deal were agreed. 'What we have been studying is what Fiat and Ford together would mean for the European market,' he told me, 'If it could be realised, which is very difficult, it would mean a stronger competitor in Europe.

In Great Britain it would mean that Ford of England would probably rationalise its product not only with Ford of Germany but even with Fiat of Italy. It would be one unit. We would have components made together, we'd have lower costs, and I think it would be an advantage for everybody including Ford of England.' By rationalisation, he meant that instead of being responsible for the sales of one and a half million cars, the newly merged company would be responsible for three million cars: it might want to make three million engines, or three million identical gearboxes, and the distribution of the work between the factories would be different. It would not mean closing Dagenham, which might for instance make the engines, while Fiat could perhaps make the gearboxes: 'On the whole rationalisation would mean that costs would be lower and that total employment would probably be lower too.'

Looking ahead to the European car industry in fifteen years time, he said that it had to be accepted that it was weaker than that of either America or Japan. In 1984, for instance, the American car industry had a profit of 10 billion dollars, and the Japanese of about 4 billion: 'The European industry algebraically summing it up had a loss of 1 billion dollars, so that shows already how much weaker we are and how much less we can invest – and this is including the Americans in Europe.' Production capacity is another problem to which he feels a solution is needed. With thirty-one million cars produced annually in the world today, he told us, there is an over-capacity of five million cars, fifty per cent of it in Europe: a European industry with two and a half million surplus cars and a loss of a billion dollars was weak.

'Then you must consider that there is no one in Europe who has more than twelve per cent of the market, and we are six companies having that share of the market,' he told us, 'If any of these six could combine and had at least twenty-five per cent of the market, that would be constructing something strong for the European industry.' Which of the six would do this, which were the most convenient, it was difficult to say. Geographically, he felt that Ford and Fiat were a very good combination. His contention that the future lay in a smaller number of head groups did not, he claimed, mean that there would not be the same trademarks: 'You'd have the same number of factories and companies but if, in Europe, these ten million cars were in the hands of two or three or four responsible groups instead of six, seven, eight or nine, surely it would be stronger.' Fiat would, of course, do its best to be part of this adventure.

The talks between Fiat and Ford had one positive outcome: the truck divisions of the two companies combined as Iveco Ford, widely advertised in 1986 as 'an equal interest partnership'. Ford's figures for the previous year give some idea of the size of the new organisation: Ford's truck exports were worth £60 million and the Ford factory at Langley in Berkshire employed 1700 people; £125 million had just been invested in a new range.

Giovanni Agnelli was sixty-five when we talked to him, but although he has the sort of face which looks as though it has lived life to the full he showed no sign of impending old age. His sister has said that he is not a happy man, because he is not at rest and cannot accept the idea of becoming old. It is perhaps that very quality of restlessness, combined with his natural charm and his indivisible loyalties to his family, his firm and his country, which has enabled him to control his destiny as the head of both a vast and influential business empire, and a family accustomed to power and leadership. So far, neither his only son, nor his younger brother, seems to have inherited his easy appearance of uncrowned royalty, and he has set no date for his abdication.

The economist J.K. Galbraith once described Giovanni Agnelli as unique among industrialists: 'His power depends on his extraordinary capacity of thinking for himself – most industrialists absorb and repeat the best contemporary clichés.' Although his charisma and elegance may seem like a cliché, in spite of a serious skiing accident a few years ago, followed a year later by a heart by-pass operation, his ability to think for himself, his energy and, of course, his charm are apparently undiminished. He still drives too fast and still dazzles his countrymen with an endless display of wealth, power and imaginative leadership.

ROBERT ANDERSON OF ARCO

CHAPTER 3

THE ENIGMATIC OIL TYCOON

When one first meets Mr Robert Anderson, it is difficult to believe that he really is the biggest private landowner in the the United States and the man who set up the Atlantic Richfield Company – ARCO – America's seventh largest oil company and tenth biggest industrial corporation. He is the man whose company made the world's biggest ever oil strike at Prudhoe Bay in Alaska. The Chairman of a Development Institute which he founded and which every year spends millions of his dollars on projects in the Third World, he is also sponsor of the Aspen Institute in Colorado, a high-powered conference centre for his internationally significant guests. He has bought and sold the *Observer* in London, has been a Director of the Chase Manhattan Bank and CBS, has set up the biggest solar energy factory in the world, and has an enviable private art collection.

Robert Anderson is a shy, soft-spoken, almost hesitant man; a mid-Westerner, he is rather like an avuncular and genial version of Winston Churchill with more of a tonsure of white hair and always a twinkle in his eye. The slightly fleshy cherubic face gives no hint of the steeliness which he has obviously needed to take him to the top; his quiet laid-back drawl is not the voice one would imagine as that of a business tycoon, a wheeler-dealer around the world, negotiating with the Chinese in Peking one minute and senior Republicans in Washington the next. Perhaps we simply all have deep-seated prejudices and preconceptions about what sort of person a successful executive ought to be: Mr Robert Anderson counfounds all these images. But his appearence is deceptive. One cannot avoid the impression that somewhere deep down a very tough and complicated man is hiding behind a mask of slightly bumbling charm.

Robert Orville Anderson was born in Chicago in 1917, the son of Hilda (née Nelson) and Hugo Anderson, a well known local banker whose family had come to the United States from Sweden, and who earned himself a revered place among the early oil prospecting businesses by lending money against proven but as yet untapped oil reserves. Robert grew up on the south side of the city in the Hyde Park-Kenwood area close to the University, and in this highly charged intellectual atmosphere was sent to a new experimental school on the campus. His education was much influenced by the Chancellor of Chicago University at the time, Robert Maynard Hutchins, who maintained that all future leaders in the country should have a broad liberal arts education deeply rooted in classical literature. Throughout his student days Robert Anderson's reading lists were heavy with philosophy and the classics. At the same time he felt that he was not cut out for city life and had developed a fascination for the outdoors; family summers were spent in Wyoming and Montana. He had already decided at that stage that he wanted to live in a small community somewhere in the West.

He graduated from Chicago in 1939 with a BA degree in Economics and in the same year married a fellow student, Barbara Phelps. His first job was with the American Mineral Spirits Company in Chicago, but he soon tired of it and less than two years later moved with his wife to start a new life in New Mexico. In 1941, 'with a wide-brimmed hat and a loan of $50,000' – his father had negotiated the money from a family friend – Mr Anderson bought a small run-down oil refinery near Artesia in New Mexico and was soon 'wild-catting', as prospecting for oil was picturesquely called. The demand for petrol and oil in the early years of the Second World War helped him to turn the refinery into an efficient and profitable enterprise. He became President of Malco Refineries Inc., which later changed to the Hondo Oil and Gas Company, and gradually prospered through a series of shrewd mergers and takeovers.

At the time he said that he was more interested in fly fishing than corporate affairs, but in fifteen years he bought and expanded six oil refineries, struck oil in a number of exploration wells and laid nearly 500 miles of oil pipeline. In 1955 he was able to use his profits to buy Wilshire Oil of California for $2 million. The company was soon restored to profitability and, in 1957, Mr Anderson sold it to Gulf Oil at a $21 million profit. He decided to diversify and bought a series of vast ranches in New Mexico and Texas on which he raised beef from a new cross-bred Angus and Brahma called a Brangus. These animals made more efficient use of the sparse grazing: they needed less fodder than any other breed to add a pound of body weight. He had a total herd of more than 30,000, and liked nothing better than riding a favourite horse on the range to look at them and the scenery in general.

By 1963 he had built the Hondo Oil and Gas company into such a strong position that it was able to merge with the Atlantic Refining Company, a deal which gave him 500,000 shares for $35 million – five per cent of the company – and a seat on the board. In 1964 he was appointed Chairman of the company's executive committee and in 1965, after the chairman at the time, Mr Henderson Supplee, had suffered a heart attack, was made Chairman and Chief Executive Officer.

He had intended to retire at about this time. With a respectable income, he could have amused himself with the life of a cattle rancher, even, perhaps as Director of the Aspen Institute for Humanistic Studies, the retreat he had funded as a forum where businessmen could be exposed to seminars and discussions with scientists, artists, scholars of all kinds and government leaders. But Mr Anderson changed his mind about early retirement from the oil industry because he realised that the company in which he now had such a large share was not performing well. As a Director of Atlantic, he realised that some radical management changes were needed if the company was to have a chance of improvement, and, naturally, he wanted to put these into effect himself.

When he came to Atlantic, the company was not sure what to make of its new boss with his drawl and his stetson. They knew that he had always been able to beat the competition to a profitable deal, make an operation work efficiently, and then get out at exactly the right moment. But he was something of an oddity when he went to board meetings at the company's head office in Philadelphia. Atlantic Refining was an elderly and respectable Eastern establishment, housed in uninspiring offices with pea-green decor and uniform oak desks. Executives rarely visited the production fields in Texas. The company was also said to be 'crude short' and vulnerable in its exclusively Eastern markets. Its stock was undervalued.

Mr Anderson was cautious about exerting his influence at his first board meetings, but soon made up his mind about what needed to be done. When he was appointed Chairman, he hired an aircraft and visited every office in the company. According to one of his colleagues, 'There was general apprehension about Anderson in management. Atlantic placed value on organisational stability and continuity. There was a feeling that he made companies work at the expense of their organisations.'

He certainly made Atlantic work. He streamlined the staff, cut the least profitable service stations and ordered a huge modernisation programme. His style is illustrated by the sort of impromptu planning session he had on a flight to London with Mr Thornton Bradshaw, the new President of the company and the man with whom he worked in tandem for the next fifteen years. Sketching out his goals for Atlantic, Mr Anderson scribbled a few points on half a sheet of paper: balance refining capacity with crude supply, avoid unstable foreign operations, expand into petrochemicals, diversify into other natural resources, and make the company bigger through mergers. It seems he has always had the ability to see wood from trees. The two men did not have to wait long for a merger opportunity.

By July 1965, Cities Service and Sinclair, the two main owners of the Richfield Oil Corporation, had been ordered by the Courts to divest their interest. Mr Anderson contacted the Chairman of Richfield, whom he had met on a fishing weekend, and arranged a meeting in a hotel in New York where a few days later the two agreed a price for Richfield. They called in a lawyer, drew up an agreement and then telephoned the President of Richfield in Los Angeles to announce the news and organise a meeting there between Mr Anderson and senior staff the following day. 'It was an extraordinary way for Atlantic to operate,' said one of their senior executives, 'it was like two Heads of State reaching a broad based decision and then telling their staff to work out the details.' Mr Anderson consolidated the management of the two firms and in 1968 moved his headquarters to New York. He said that he thought the company ought to be moved into a 'more active business atmosphere, closer to some of the other oil companies; New York seemed logical, and any change shakes things up a little.'

The most significant addition to the new company's fortunes came with Richfield's drilling and exploration leases in the North Slope oil field in Alaska. Many other oil companies had been prospecting there for a number of years, but most had recently become disillusioned and had withdrawn. Mr Anderson had an intuition that Atlantic Richfield, ARCO, should continue drilling, and in 1968 his confidence and patience were rewarded. The geologists' report on their tests was more optimistic than anyone could have hoped. He was able to announce that ARCO had discovered reserves at Prudhoe Bay in Alaska in what was soon to be recognised as the world's biggest ever oil strike. As a direct result of ARCO's find, America's proven oil resources had been doubled overnight. Today, Mr Anderson looks back at this achievement and his relentless ascent of the corporate ladder with a detached modesty.

I asked him to describe his job and what priorities he had in running a company and making business decisions. 'My role is trying to steer the company in a long range sense and to make policy decisions and plans for the future growth of the company,' he said. The company was totally dependent on the people that it could attract and hold, and to have an exciting company meant being able to attract much better people, hold their attention and give them better careers: 'You shouldn't be so intrusive that you preclude their own independent thinking, because that is something you very much want to encourage,' Mr Anderson told me, 'But still they should know your general feelings on certain subjects.' He thought that the character of the Chief Executive was reflected throughout an entire organisation. It was important to show interest in his people and in the company and its products, although there were times when he might have concerns which he could not share: 'Sometimes there are problems that are so big you just don't want to bother the others with them.' He was not, he said, thinking of company secrets but just general problems: 'A general of an army who is in an impossible situation could not let his army or his field people know, no matter how bad it was.' Fortunately, however, the company had no such problems when we met: he was 'very comfortable with our people and with what they are doing' and had never had a better team – and as he had seen a lot of them himself he felt he was in a pretty good position to judge.

What qualities did he look for when he was choosing senior managers? 'It is very important that they should understand what the problem is and what they are trying to do,' he said, 'and, if possible, have had experience in it. It is not always possible to get people who are experienced in a field but they should have enough related experience to make them able to step into it. You need someone who will really work, and in the top positions of a company that takes tremendous stamina.' He did not think people realised the physical stamina required of an executive in a top position. His day was apt to be endless, and demands on him were difficult to predict. He considered that the ability to get along with people and concern for his fellow employees – particularly those working under him – was a very important factor, because those people could not perform unless there was some rapport and respect: 'People under him have to feel free to communicate with him. The executive with a terrible temper can't produce because the people under him are stifled.' It is difficult to imagine Robert Anderson losing his temper.

His own stamina has been well tested. He has had to put in a day's work and then think nothing of having to travel for another five or six hours to get ready for another day's work, and to accept a great variety of pressures, both internal and external. Oil is, as he explained, a very international business; it is constantly under market pressures and constitutes the largest commodity market in the world: 'You have to be conversant with what is going on in the market place, with your competitors globally, and you have to know what the market is in Rotterdam, Houston, or Singapore.' He told me that he had travelled, on average, about 500 to 600 miles a day every day of his life for the last forty years. That year (1985) had been particularly busy, and he expected to travel between 250,000 and 300,000 miles. He had made a four-day trip to Peking the previous week, as well as a three-day trip to London, which was longer than usual. 'Most of these trips to New York or anywhere are just literally overnight trips so there's not much pleasure in that kind of travel,' he pointed out, 'You're tied up for breakfast, lunch and dinner and, as soon as you're finished, you're loading up and late evening you're flying someplace else.'

Had it not been for the Alaskan oil strike, Mr Anderson might have remained the successful boss of a middle-sized company. He had clearly enjoyed applying himself to the problems of Atlantic and had been successful with his new management ideas. He told us that he had obviously wanted to succeed in whatever he was doing in business, but had never had an over-riding ambition to be the head of a large international corporation. What catapulted him into prominence was that one single find, so large that it is difficult to appreciate its significance. I asked him whether it had been the result of acute, careful planning or just luck: 'Both, I'd say – ninety per cent luck and ten per cent acute, careful planning.' Statistically, he assessed the chance of finding an oil field that size from any given exploratory well as like winning the Irish sweepstakes – 'and I don't think you could say that you could win the Irish sweepstakes by acute planning.' He had just been extraordinarily fortunate and described himself as 'an old wildcatter who has spent his life looking for oil'. 'That was the greatest discovery in this hemisphere,' he said; it was going to take years and years to develop fully and play its role out, but before that was over it was not inconceivable that it could ultimately produce revenues close to a trillion dollars. This would have an enormous impact on the country's trade balances: 'The replacement factor, if we had to import it, would run into billions of dollars annually, so from a national viewpoint it's a very major economic factor.' Already, he estimated, it was saving about $20 billion a year in America's balance of payments simply having that field in Alaska – 'About half our Japanese deficit is right there.'

Immediately after the Alaskan strike, Mr Anderson got wind that one of his competitors, Gulf and Western, was about to make an offer for the Sinclair Oil Company. This was too good an opportunity to miss, but he knew that he would have to act quickly. 'We saw this as filling in the gap between the East and West coasts,' he said in an interview at the time. 'We were going to have a lot of oil coming out of Alaska and this was the first time we had considered going from a company that had 400,000 barrels of refining [capacity] to double that.' The head of Sinclair, Mr Pen Thomas, was very receptive to his proposal and over dinner they agreed broad terms. The next day Mr Anderson went off on a family trekking holiday in the West, leaving instructions with a negotiating team in case an agreement had to be made in his absence.

A few days later he telephoned his office from a coin box in the middle of nowhere, and learned that ARCO had just arranged a $432 million revolving bank credit within two days to back its bid for Sinclair shares. The merger added Alaska's Kuparuk oil field, a refinery in Houston, a pipeline system, petrochemicals, various properties in Indonesia, and market- ing and production organisations in the middle of the conti- nent. In total, the two mergers, Richfield and Sinclair, had tripled the size of the original Atlantic Refining company. The production of crude oil, the number of service stations and the volume of sales had all tripled as well.

Billions of dollars flooded into ARCO's coffers. The company was awash with cash. Dividends were raised and, after tax, there were new operations and new investment. ARCO built a fleet of supertankers which plied between a terminal in Alaska at the end of a company pipeline and ARCO's refineries on the West Coast. The pipeline, although undoubtedly something of an engineering miracle, was strongly opposed by all the environmental groups, and Mr Anderson commissioned a specialist photographer to prove that it had not damaged the wildlife. He decided to move the company headquarters from New York to two huge office towers in Flower Street in downtown Los Angeles. He himself had a special suite on the fifty-first floor of the block, overlooking the offices of all his rivals and associates as well as their rooftop gardens, swimming pools and helicopter pads: the boss of ARCO could look down on them all.

The Niagara of incoming cash was disposed of in many other ways. His vastly increased personal wealth was gradually invested in a series of ranches in Texas and New Mexico which eventually had a total area of more than a million acres, and made him the biggest private landowner in the country. He had more than 30,000 head of cattle and at least 10,000 sheep on such properties as the Diamond A Ranch or the Circle Diamond, Latigo, Ladder, Four Dinkus, Squaw Canyon and many others with equally picturesque names.

But not all of his enterprises were as successful as he would have liked. He invested in a farming scheme in Iran, for example, not realising until it was too late that the Shah would soon be toppled and his money inevitably lost. He was also tempted to put money into a vast speculative agricultural scheme in Brazil, the Jari forestry and pulp project, which had been set up by an octogenarian American multi-millionaire, Daniel Ludwig, reputedly the richest man in the world.

ARCO agreed to put money into the scheme because it wanted to investigate whether it would be possible to constitute petrol from the rice which was to be grown in the Amazon jungle. The whole project foundered in bureaucracy, an inhospitable climate, poor management and low prices, and had to be rescued by a consortium of twenty-three banks and private companies with help from the Brazilian Government. Mr Ludwig himself appears to have lost $1000 million.

But for every mistake or unlucky deal, Mr Anderson had a dozen which worked somewhat more successfully. He bought and sold banks and businesses, property and developments throughout the West, and added horses and a wide variety of paintings to his favourite family residence near Roswell in New Mexico.

It was there that he and his wife Barbara brought up their two sons and five daughters. Their children are all grown up now, some with children themselves, but each Thanksgiving

Day most of them manage to assemble for a family reunion at the house in New Mexico. There are family portraits in oils, group photographs by the pool, and in the grounds a restored Mexican chapel, where many of the children were married and the grandchildren christened, has been rebuilt under groups of flowering trees. In a corner of the private chapel the names of Katherine, Julia, Maria, Robert, William, Barbara and Beverley are woven into a carpet tapestry designed by the Austrian artist and friend of the family, Herbert Bayer.

At the Circle Diamond Ranch, I talked to Robert and Barbara Anderson in a room at the top of the house filled with his personal collection of Indian artefacts. When I asked Mrs Anderson what she thought was the secret of her husband's success, she told me that it was his uncanny business sense, an extraordinary intuition which cannot be explained. 'He constantly amazes me by knowing things he has no way of knowing,' she said.

It is at the ranch that Robert Anderson seems to be happiest, far from his Los Angeles headquarters; he likes to ride alone on the range, the owner of all he surveys, occasionally dropping in to chat with his cowhands about the progress of the latest beef rearing scheme. He is fond of the argument so often deployed by those with large landholdings, that they are merely trustees or stewards for future generations, and says that it is his duty to make sure that it is properly cared for and not overgrazed. 'This is mine at the moment,' he told me, waving a hand at the sand-coloured hills, 'but many others will own it in the future.'

His apparently deep concern for environmental matters has been another outlet for ARCO's new wealth, through a variety of humanitarian, cultural and development projects which he has decided to support. Twenty years after his university education with its emphasis on noble motives, he was able to practise on the grandest scale what had been preached to him as a student. He set up the International Institute for Environment and Development with offices in Washington, London, Paris and Buenos Aires. He was the original benefactor of the Aspen Institute for Humanistic Studies in the skiing resort of Aspen, Colorado, which was set up as 'a forum whose goal is to initiate and enlarge discussions on the major issues of the time'. The ARCO Foundation has given grants worth several million dollars every year to projects ranging from the improvement of housing conditions among America's inner city poor to the sponsorship of young up-coming painters and photographers.

Mr Anderson suprised many of his colleagues by also contributing to environmental groups. Some of these, although they accepted his generosity, were cynical about ARCO's motives. Mr Don May of the Los Angeles branch of Friends of the Earth told us, 'One of the things under our system which a corporate executive tries to do is influence the regulators of his industry – and Anderson does a very effective job of that. He's a tough competitor, but he plays by the rules.' When there have been formal hearings to decide whether a permit should be granted for oil or gas exploration, ARCO, we were told, has come well prepared with a large corporation staff of lawyers and research staff. They make concessions which are commensurate with the profit they have to give their stockholders, Mr May said, but, unlike some other large oil companies in California, they do at least go through the proceedings.

When I asked Mr Anderson why he had given so much money to environmental groups, he said he saw it as a proper function of his corporation: 'We believe environmental problems like air and water pollution are real and genuine. We think some are far more important than others but, nevertheless, that there is a legitimate basis for the environmental movement and that a corporation like ours has to show concern for the problems which are endemic to our society.' He did not accept that he was also, at the same time, trying to buy off criticism by giving money to environmentalists. 'No, no,' he insisted, 'I know enough about the environmental groups to know that you can't buy them off in any form.' There had, he told us, never been any time when he had hoped to improve his lot with them by supporting them, and the company often found itself just as much at odds with them as ever.

He saw no contradiction between someone who claimed to be concerned about the environment also being head of a company which was exploiting the environment, because he considered it essential to resolve environmental problems simultaneously with economic development. 'If we do not have continuing economic development and growth in the world, the outlook for future generations is going to be extremely bleak,' he told us, 'We have to resolve these environmental problems and still provide job opportunities for a better way of life to a future generation if we are to discharge the basic responsibility of a society like ours.'

It could not be denied, however, that the oil industry had to some extent contributed to the environmental problems, but although he agreed that the industry's products were, of course, burned and created 'air emissions and so on', he pointed out that an oil well did not make a major impact on land and was temporary: his effect on the environment could therefore be considered as transient as his ownership of vast acreages of land. 'When the well is depleted, it's abandoned and leaves very little lasting evidence,' he said. He admitted that as oil floats on the water 'we do see evidence of it occasionally on beaches and places where we don't really want to see it', but basically he did not see the oil industry as a major polluter other than in the consumption of its products: 'These are of course vital to feeding ourselves, and maintaining our society and jobs, and so on. Any human activity has an element of pollution.'

I asked him how worried he was that he was the head of a very large oil corporation in a country which used such a very large proportion of the world's available energy. 'We do use a disproportionate amount of the world's energy,' he agreed, 'and we have a significantly higher standard of living than most of the world.' Unfortunately the two were, he conceded, to a great extent connected, and he found it very difficult to conceive how the present standard of living could be maintained without continuing to consume fairly large quantities of energy. He suggested that nuclear energy might be the solution: 'Nuclear energy from my own point of view is relatively clean and the radiation problem, I believe, is containable,' he told us. 'Air and water pollution are two areas of considerable concern to me personally, and nuclear energy does not generally pollute either the air or water.' (Only a few months after this conversation, a major accident at Russia's Chernobyl nuclear plant was to cast considerable doubt on the environmental advisability of nuclear power.)

For the present, Mr Anderson was concerned, but not unduly worried, about the effect which his company might have had on the environment: he felt that any damage done could be remedied and assured us that 'We make a major effort to hold our environmental impact problems to an absolute minimum.' His competitors and adversaries all seem to agree that his concern for the environment is sincere, although one of the union spokesmen I met did point out that his approach did no harm to the corporation's public relations and probably saved money in the long term.

One ARCO adventure which neither made money, nor had any long-term effect on the environment, was the purchase of the London *Observer*. In 1976, at a time when the Alaskan millions were starting to flow, Mr Anderson rescued the paper with a package worth about $10 million. The deal was controversial at the time, but even more so was his sale of the paper, five years later, to Lonrho. Both transactions had the Anderson style – smooth, personal and decisive. He told me that he had bought the paper to re-establish links with Britain at a time when the corporation was looking for investment opportunities and the oil and gas business appeared somewhat limited.

At the time, he was quoted as saying that the purchase was 'a modest bet on the survival of England', and that he had no intention of changing the paper's editorial policy. 'Our sole intention', he said, ' was to provide support for one of the world's outstanding newspapers.' Other contemporary news reports described him in gushing terms as a 'humanist with a deep concern for communications' and a 'liberal intellectual acting out of noble motives'. I asked Mr Anderson whether he'd sold the paper because it had been a financial headache. 'Not really,' he said. 'Financially speaking, I would say we did as well as anyone's done on Fleet Street in recent years.'

Although he did not lose a great deal of money by buying and selling the *Observer*, he did not make any either. His chief reason for reselling it so swiftly was his realisation that unless there were some basic change within the unions, and in their attitude towards the paper, he saw very little future for it. The *Observer* could, he was convinced, be printed very effectively and be a very profitable paper if modern technology could be applied to it. But as work regulations and the practices in Fleet Street made it impossible to modernise plant and equipment, he felt that sooner or later either the paper would have to go out of existence, or there would have to be a major improvement in productivity in the printing plant. Although he had been aware of these factors when he bought the paper, neither he nor his associates had realised how truly inflexible the labour situation was.

Mr Anderson sold the *Observer* without consulting the editor about his decision. 'Selling a paper is a very delicate affair,' he explained, 'You cannot go around publicly announcing that a newspaper is for sale. You have to find a buyer who is interested, because there is no such thing as a secret in a newspaper. They are not supposed to have secrets – so you can't take anyone into your confidence, so to speak.' There were, inevitably, some people on the paper who more than slightly resented the way it was sold, but looking back, he did not see any other way in which it could have been done: rumours about the sale would, he felt, have been infinitely more destructive than the way it was sold. The venture into Fleet Street may not have been one of Mr Anderson's more successful enterprises, but he assured us most emphatically that he had never regretted having owned it.

It was another investment venture which put more strain on ARCO than anything else, when Mr Anderson's business intuition let him down over his hunch to buy the Anaconda mining company. Overnight, ARCO doubled the length of its payroll from 25,000 to 50,000 workers and was soon entangled in the grip of a giant the company had cause to resent. Had ARCO been smaller it might have been crushed.

Anaconda's industrial coils encircled projects in many different parts of the world. It had two subsidiaries in Chile, aluminium plants in Jamaica, Canada and Mexico, all with profits and sales which were expected to continue rising throughout the 1970s. ARCO had no experience of mining, but wanted to extract oil from shale in various sites which included an Anaconda mine in Colorado for an investment of three billion dollars. ARCO, which wanted to be at the front of the race for alternative sources of energy when oil began to diminish, needed the know-how and experience which it was thought would come from Anaconda's purchase. But Mr Anderson could hardly have picked a worse time for his first venture into such new territory.

The exchange rate made the scheme uncompetitive, the shale idea had to be dropped and the entire project was eventually written off. One investment analyst I talked to in New York estimated that the Anaconda adventure had cost ARCO more than two and a half billion dollars. Mr Anderson has somehow been able to shrug off the loss as something one should put down to experience. There are perhaps few businessmen anywhere in the world who would feel able to do that with a three billion dollar mistake.

'At the time we bought Anaconda we were convinced, along with a large number of other people in the industry, that the development of shale oil in Colorado was imminent', he explained. He anticipated at that time that by 1985 they would be mining about 150,000 tons of shale oil a day from a mine which would have been the largest of its kind in the world by a factor of two or three. Having no experience whatsoever in mining – and the costs being very critical to the success of a three billion dollar investment – he felt that they could not undertake an operation on such a large scale without having some absolutely top flight expertise in mining. It was, he explained, the desire to acquire a knowlegeable mining base, far more than a desire to get into copper or minerals, that was the motivation, although there was an attraction to the other minerals 'because of our earth orientation'. The project had subsequently been liquidated and sold, he said, because shale oil was in fact probably still thirty or forty years away.

The venture had, however, not, he assured me, been as big and expensive a mistake as it could have been if they had gone ahead with the mine: 'Hindsight is great. If we had known that the shale era would never materialise, and that the shale industry would be delayed indefinitely, we would have taken a considerably more thoughtful look at getting into it; so hindsight is great – you can always see what you shouldn't have done.' But to open the largest mine in the world without any mining experience would have taken what he termed an irresponsible brashness.

He attributed at least part of the blame for the failure of the scheme to the American government for allowing the US dollar to rise to a level which made a lot of mining operations totally uncompetitive in world markets: all the mining products were world commodities.' If anyone had been able to predict at that time that the US government would permit the US dollar to rise to its present level – we wouldn't have done it,' he said. 'With the dollar literally doubling in value against other currencies in the interval, it simply meant that there was no possible way to mine in this country and compete on a world market.' There were already high wage rates and very stringent environmental standards in a high cost producing country, he pointed out: 'But if on top of that you slap on a currency factor which is the equivalent of a fifty or sixty per cent export tax, you're just out of business.'

His complaints about unfavourable exchange rates echoed Sir John Harvey-Jones' criticisms. For the last four years, Mr Anderson said, he had been advocating that unless the dollar was brought into more competitive relationships with other currencies, America would end up a nation of fast-food vendors and entertainment manufacturers. The USA had already practically lost its steel industry, most of its heavy equipment and machinery industry and, with textiles long gone, was in the process of dismantling a large part of the agricultural base because its commodities were not competitive in the world market. 'The high dollar has been an extremely destructive factor in this country, much more than I think Washington realises,' he said, 'I have a constant on-going war with Washington over monetary policy.'

ARCO's mining losses were followed by the oil crisis of 1973, a slump in petrochemicals, over-capacity in refining and a fall in demand. The effect of these problems gradually increased over five years, but the company was by then so cumbersome that the corporation could not, it seemed, easily adapt to or recognise new emergencies. It was as if it had become a victim of its own success, and there was growing talk that it might soon be ripe for a take-over.

The man most often named in connection with this rumour was Mr T. Boone Pickens jr, the head of the relatively small Mesa Petroleum company of Amarillo in Texas. Mr Pickens, apart from having a memorable name, was the most feared and famous example of what Wall Street called a 'corporate raider', and had concentrated on looking for take-overs. His technique was to buy stock in a vulnerable company, usually in secret and on a large scale, and then profit greatly from the subsequent market trends. In 1984/5, for instance, he made more than $20 million from his skilful manipulations, and qualified for the title of the most highly paid executive in the world. (It was perhaps this scale of reward which Sir John Harvey-Jones had in mind when he had at the same time to defend a somewhat smaller salary increase in London as Chairman of the more significant ICI.)

It is all but impossible for ordinary mortals to comprehend how Mr T. Boone Pickens jr, who insists on his full name although the jr is probably optional, operates or makes his money. I first met him in a suite in a lavish hotel in the middle of Chicago; he was stretched out in an easy chair making a series of long distance telephone calls which were ticked off against a list prepared by an extremely efficient assistant. Mr T. Boone Pickens enjoys a legendary reputation, particularly in the American business press, and is sensitive about his image. He protested vehemently when a British reporter wrote an article about him and with a patronising heavy-handedness rendered his quiet Texan accent into deliberately tortured English prose. He objected too when another British reporter, who should have known better, said that an oil field in the North Sea had been called the Beatrice Field because it was a present to his wife. It was all a bit unfair and silly, and someone else might have ignored the affair. Mr T. Boone Pickens jr, however, is not a man to overlook detail.

His take-over schemes, incomprehensible to anyone out-side city circles, have been executed with meticulous planning; assistants have acted on secret instructions and at a prearranged signal have bought shares at a dozen different places under different names so that no one on Wall Street would be able to sniff what the great player was up to. He was only interested, he told us, in improving the lot of the average stock holder. All his financial manoeuvrings were aimed solely at that target.

As far as I know, he has never admitted in public that he ever planned a take-over of ARCO; but that is certainly what many others in the industry, including journalists, ARCO executives and the ARCO unions, believed he was up to. I asked him whether a company like ARCO could be vulnerable to a 'raider'. 'Anybody can be vulnerable to a raider, don't make any difference who it is,' he said, 'If their stock is selling at a deep discount to appraised value, then there's the opportunity there and the money, and you can go out and get money to make these deals. So, if the money is there and the discount is deep enough, the opportunity does exist and the probability is there, and consequently something can happen. It's the job of management to get the price up – that's what they're hired to do. Why do you think anyone goes out and buys a share of stock? Because they want to make money and its up to the management of the company to be sure that they make money by raising the price of the stock.'

In 1984, although ARCO was reluctant to voice in public any fears about the dreaded Boone Pickens and a possible take-over, Mr Anderson decided that he would have to act quickly if a financial crisis were to be avoided. He drew up a so-called restructuring plan which drastically pruned the company. The workforce was to be cut in three years from 55,000 to 25,000. Staff were offered voluntary redundancy. Luxury activities, not directly concerned with raising revenue, were to go: there were to be no more genteel departments for the purchasing of trendy modern paintings for the ARCO gallery. Oil exploration and development projects were contracted or postponed, and loss-making non-oil projects were written off at a total cost of $1.3 billion. The most radical of all these measures, however, was Mr Anderson's financial juggling. The ARCO Towers headquarters in Los Angeles were sold to help repurchase $4 billion of ARCO's own stock and thus increase the value of the company.

Mr Anderson is still able to describe the whole trauma with a laconic detatchment. 'It's a massive saving and reduction in manpower; our earnings will show a substantial benefit from this reduction. Most of those very high quality and high paying jobs will not be replaced,' he told us. When I asked him whether he felt guilty that he had got rid of so many jobs at a time of growing unemployment in the country generally, he admitted that he had mixed emotions about it: 'As skipper of the ship, I have to do what is necessary, but I question whether this in the long run is truly in the national interest.' But he was convinced that there was no question about the benefit to shareholders; ARCO will be a stronger company and from his point of view as head of the company it made great sense. The moves were, he told us, well thought out and planned: some went back eight or ten years, so 'it was not a rash move at all.'

He nevertheless hated to see his country creating circumstances that forced him into such drastic action. 'The decision on our part,' he explained, 'was a result of US monetary and economic policy – no question of that. The irony is that most of the various businesses we've disposed of played a major role in the defence of this country in World War Two. It does not seem to bother Washington that we can no longer supply strategic materials in this country. It does not seem to bother them that what we are doing will greatly aggravate our balance of payments problems, because what we have elected not to do will have to be replaced by imports.' Washington should, he warned, wake up to the fact that keeping people employed was the number one business of the government – or any other government in the world – and that America had 'the highest levels of the aggregate of unemployment': 'There is nothing in the last fifty years to rival the unemployment problem which we have today.'

The unions at ARCO were not consulted about the restructuring until Mr Anderson's plans had been put into effect: they were merely officially informed later. One cannot help gaining the impression that the unions in the American oil business do not have all that much influence anyway. We found Mr Jack Foley of the Union of Oil, Chemical and Atomic

Workers, for instance, in an undistinguished office block on the Long Beach Boulevard, part of an anonymous Los Angeles suburb.

Mr Foley was friendly, open and talkative, but did not exactly radiate an air of forcefulness. Of course he would have liked to have been consulted about the ARCO restructuring plan, he said, and would have wanted to find other ways of achieving the same results. Had he been consulted, he would, he claimed, have tried to convince the company that some of the things they wanted to sell should have been kept, or that the changes should have put into effect over a longer period. When I asked him what chance he thought he had of saving jobs which Mr Anderson wanted to lose, he conceded that he did not have the slightest chance: 'I think those jobs are probably gone.' I asked him why he thought ARCO was reducing staff. 'I think the threat of a T. Boone Pickens type of arrangement was on the cards,' he said. 'They probably felt vulnerable; I believe they really felt that somebody like T. Boone Pickens could have made a take-over bid. I think they had a large amount of stock out there; their debt level was high; I don't believe they felt they could operate the total expanse of that corporation with the amount of crude they had guaranteed by using all the refinery facilities.'

When I asked Mr Anderson how much say he allowed the unions to have in the debate about job losses, he looked a little vague and finally conceded only that the company had worked with the unions on the 'termination agreements'. Judging from the way he went about things during the controversial sale of the *Observer*, he is not in the habit of consulting anyone else if he can avoid it. The Anderson manner may seem soft, charming and bedside-like, but there is not much room for sentiment behind it, and the unions, one imagines, were generally considered either irrelevant or an avoidable nuisance.

'We consulted, obviously, over retirement plans,' Mr Anderson told me. 'I think they were aware that we were confronted with problems. You take the Anaconda mine at Bute in Montana; it has world class deposits, it's one of the great mines in the world, but it could not operate in today's economic climate, and the unions were advised three or four years in advance that it was just a question of time before it would have to be closed.' When I put it to him that we had been told that unions in the oil industry in the United States did not really have any effect and could be ignored by the leaders of the industry, he not surprisingly objected to such an interpretation. 'It isn't that,' he said, 'I'd say we have very effective unions. The relationship between the unions and companies has usually been excellent because working conditions are considered to be high.' But he admitted that 'certain parts are not unionised at all – where you get oil fields and the dispersal of workers.'

To a question about whether he thought the unions were strong enough, he did give a surprising answer: 'I think they are strong enough, but they are losing strength. Henry Ford changed the world even more than Napoleon when he went down to his plant one day and discovered that none of his Ford workers was driving a Ford car because he couldn't afford one. He said "the people who build my cars should be able to afford my cars," so he ordered that everyone's pay should be doubled right then. When he did that he created a greater revolution in the twentieth century than any other man who has ever lived on this planet, because he made the working man the consumer. Our consuming class today is the rank and file. When you put a working man in a position where he can become a purchaser of his own, then you have a strong viable economy. Henry Ford is the man who doubled the wages and set a pattern which the rest of the world followed.'

He was not, however, thinking of following Henry Ford's example by doubling the wages of ARCO's employees: it would not work today, he said, you'd have to be Henry Ford. 'He did that one thing, and that is the reason I say that unions can play a very important role, because they have helped to see that a reasonable amount of the national wealth is being distributed to the workers.' He thought it fair to say that this would probably have happened anyway, but felt that the union movement had done a great deal to distribute income in the country in a way that supported its economic interest.

In the event, Mr T. Boone Pickens jr was not able to close his fingers around the tantalising ARCO prize – if indeed that had ever been his goal; one can never be sure in these matters. But he certainly had some strong views on the outcome and of what he thought should happen in the market for shares in the bigger oil companies:'If you look at the ten largest oil companies selling at fifty per cent of appraised value, if those managements could get the price of their stock from fifty to seventy five per cent of appraised value, four million stockholders in the United States would make seventy billion dollars.' ARCO had, he considered, taken the first step to moving their price closer to appraised value, and over a period of time there would be other steps to accomplish what had to be done; the stockholders, whose interests are of course always uppermost in his mind, would demand it.

I asked him to elaborate on the steps he thought should or would be taken: 'Well, you've already seen other things in the past, Royalty Trusts, Master limited partnerships. There are going to be other spin-offs and divestures of assets and a greater distribution of proceeds to stockholders. Dividends will be raised, stock buy-backs will take place. What we're going to see is that the companies get progressively smaller.'

When I asked him what the restructuring of ARCO had done for the shareholders, T. Boone Pickens jr assumed that I would recall that when it was announced, it had two parts – the restructuring itself, and the announcement of the loss in the first quarter of the year of 1 billion 200 million dollars. 'Have you ever heard of a company, in a matter of a week after an announcement that would be devastating to the extent of $1 billion 200 million, have at the same time an increase in the value of their stock?' he asked, 'The value of the stock went up in one week 1 billion 500 million dollars.' It went up, he explained, because ARCO was getting ready for the share buy-back from the stockholders and was going to raise the dividend. It was all going to enhance the value for the stockholders, he explained, and so the price went up. He was sure ARCO's management was absolutely delighted, but implied that there was little difference between what they had done and his own method of operating. 'If you go back and look at the five deals that we were involved in – City Service, General American, Gulf, Phillips and Unical – these five companies had 750,000 stockholders,' he told me, 'and the market enhancement that we put into those companies was described by some people as paper profits. Well, if cheques are paper profits, that is exactly what happened.

Nothing fundamental had happened to the companies' capacity to actually produce things, I suggested; surely he was just talking about financial adjustments. 'We made the market place recognise the values and those stockholders made $13 billion,' he explained, 'That is not insignificant. It was not the overall purchase of those assets; it was the pre-tax profit on them, money which went back into the economy. The Federal Government picked up more than $3 billion in tax on that money.' ARCO had done something similar: 'They have created up to $3 billion in values for their stockholders in a year, because they have made the market place recognise the value of the underlying assets.'

Mr Anderson justified the extraordinary financial juggling with ARCO shares as a 'tough judgement call' and the result of a decision to do everything possible to enhance earnings while paying less attention to long range plans. 'A large company must perform at optimum level if it is to avoid the T. Boone Pickens's of the world', he said, 'In other words if management can't do it somebody else is going to step in and take over, and that is the way it should be'. When I asked Mr Anderson his opinion of T. Boone Pickens, he laughed and described him as 'a charming guy, a delightful shooting companion anywhere and very shrewd and tough'. But he had reservations about Mr Pickens' real motives in attempting take-overs: 'I do question in my own mind whether he ever really wants to catch one of these fish. He likes to angle for them but I think he makes so much money angling that I'm not sure he ever really wants to catch one.' He had a feeling that if T. Boone Pickens ever caught one of the fish, he might discover that it was more of a problem than he had anticipated and that it was 'easier to steer from the outside than to do so from the inside'.

'He may have snapped a few sleepy managements together and I'd say that's good,' Mr Anderson told me, 'But some of the companies he has made a run at have been left in very difficult circumstances. In trying to avoid him, some of the companies have acquired debts and done other things which would not have been done normally in business. It will take them some years to recover from some of the manoeuvres. For the companies, it has probably been traumatic, to put it mildly, but a little trauma now and then is not all that bad'. He agreed that Mr Pickens' claim that his main concern was solely the interest of the shareholders was a pretty accurate statement 'because after all he is a shareholder, so if he says his interest is the shareholders' it sort of fits – it happens to be T. Boone's himself'.

Mr Anderson has often been described as a man for whom there is no sentiment in business: this was certainly displayed in the revolution he brought about in ARCO. His Chief Executive, for instance, Mr Bill Kieschnick, was to be entrusted with the task of putting the restructuring plan into effect, but had reservations about its wisdom and said so in a board meeting. He soon found that he had been included in the list of redundancies, after nearly forty years' service. No one could accuse ARCO of keeping one corner of the company insulated from the freezing draughts.

At the same time, ARCO decided to get out of the oil business in the east of the country altogether. Mr Anderson agreed to withdraw from all petrol refining and marketing east of the Mississipi, and concentrate instead on the more profitable business in the west of the United States, where ARCO faced less competition. Chains of service stations disappeared, while in California the remainder were developed into combined service stations and minimarkets open twenty-four hours a day. The marketing technique pioneered by ARCO brought increased customers and turnover and was soon copied by competitors.

Because of all the policy changes, there were some observers of the oil industry who began to whisper that the all-seeing Bob Anderson had made a particularly significant discovery, and deduced from the extensive restructuring that the old wildcatter was secretly intent on getting out of oil altogether. After all was it not true that ARCO was the biggest producer in the world of solar panels? Mr Anderson himself seemed scandalised that anyone should have suggested that he was taking the first steps to get out of his favourite commodity. 'Our strategy is to concentrate on oil,' he told us. 'But we are not particularly interested in refining oil beyond our own in-house oil.'

When I suggested that he was not as committed to oil as before he replied, 'If anyone thinks we're getting out of oil, they've got us going in the wrong direction. We have extraordinarily good reserves, second to no one in the private industries. We still have tremendous known deposits of oil in the Arctic and we are more of an oil producing company than any major oil company. The reduction of our oil and gas exploration programme in this country does not mean any reduced interest in exploration. We're simply going to be more selective about it. We are discovering much more oil per dollar expended outside the United States than inside, and we are going to put more emphasis on foreign exploration.'

If oil were a finite substance, how much longer did he think the oil industry had a real future? There was no more oil in the world than was thought ten years ago, he said, but world demand had been much slower than anticipated, and as a result it would last longer because consumption was lower than it had been. He was, however, convinced that there was no question that eventually a point would be reached when there was a shortage of petroleum. It would not be in the near term – the Middle East reserves were still enormous – but the rest of the world was no more than holding its own in producing oil; once the Middle East's reserves began to decline, then the rest of the world would face a diminishing supply. 'My own theory of the schedule is that we are in very comfortable shape for the next five or six years,' he told us, 'and in pretty good shape until the end of the century but I would say that in twenty-five or thirty years we could have some serious problems. But I don't see any near term supply problem. Our Alaskan position is that we have at least twenty years more development.'

Although he felt it was true that overall oil was a declining industry, people in it, himself included, had been saying to themselves for the last twenty years that some day the oil would be gone 'and we'll have to learn to do something else':

'Well, we've tried that and we haven't done very well doing anything else.' Because of the Alaskan discoveries, ARCO would, he was convinced, be able to remain an active oil company longer than some of the others, although he admitted that 'If you are in an industry and you know there is an end to it at some point, it begins to affect your employees.' By the time the oil industry started to slow down, he thought that some form of electric driving mechanism for vehicles would have been perfected, and that nuclear power would continue to take a larger share of electric power generation.

In spite of Mr Anderson's insistence that his company is fully committed to oil, he is also putting considerable effort into solar energy. ARCO is the largest manufacturer in the world of solar equipment, but he considers this relatively insignificant as he claims it amounts only to about one hundredth of one per cent of the company's sales. So although I suggested that they were putting a tremendous amount into it, he would admit only: 'We're giving it an honest try but it's a teeny part of our company.' Some day, he thought, solar energy might become a major part, but at present it was a very small part, more of a dream and a research effort than a reality.

Mr Anderson is unduly modest about ARCO's solar effort. Considerable resources have been pumped into the research projects at a laboratory in California, and his solar cells are being marketed all over the world. But at the same time it is true that ARCO is far from abandoning the black gold which until now has been the source of the company's wealth. For several years Mr Anderson has been competing with the other major American oil companies, for instance, for a share of the huge oil prospecting prize in the South China Sea – an oil field which is thought to have perhaps twice the resources of the North Sea.

For three decades the Chinese prospected unsuccessfully for oil themselves, mainly in their oil fields at Daqing and in the Taklimakan Desert in Xin Kiang. They then invited the West to help: Mr Anderson knew a good business opportunity when he saw one. In 1982, in the Hall of the People in Peking, he signed an agreement which allowed ARCO to explore 3500 square miles of the South China Sea, south of Hainan Island; if oil were found they were to share the development costs and the proceeds with the Chinese. In that case it was estimated that ARCO would be spending $2.5 billion over thirty-five years. It was the first exploration agreement between the Chinese and a major western oil company and by far the biggest. Once again, the old wildcatter was playing a hunch. It will be some time before we will know whether he has been lucky here too. But as Mr T. Boone Pickens jr said when he asked his opinion of Robert Anderson as a businessman, 'You judge a trapper by his pelts – and he's got pelts.'

Because of his international experience and his influence in the industry at large, Mr Anderson's views are widely sought and listened to. He is one of the biggest private contributors to the Republican Party, and has contacts in Washington at the highest level. Early in 1986 he announced that he was stepping down from the Chairmanship of ARCO, but he has retained his seat on the board as well as all his shares and ranches. Many in the American oil industry have a suspicion that Mr Robert Anderson will continue to be the guiding force behind the company he founded for a good many years.

In many ways, Robert Anderson is the most enigmatic of the six industrialists on whom this series of portraits is based. In a country where business success is often depicted as the fruit of ruthless energy, toughness and ambition, he does not seem to fit into any of the stereotypes. He looks more like an old-fashioned cowboy than a business tycoon, and his geniality and slow-spoken charm have certainly helped to capitalise on his amazingly fortunate business intuition. His record of concern about the environment and international questions goes beyond the usual preoccupations of the businessman and puts him in a class of his own. Like Sir John Harvey-Jones and Giovanni Agnelli, however, he has proved himself capable of being tough, uncompromising and brutally realistic in the interests of his beloved oil business.

AKIO MORITA OF SONY

CHAPTER 4

JAPAN'S SUPER SALESMAN

Mr Akio Morita is Chairman, Chief Executive Officer and co-founder of the Japanese electronics firm, Sony, and is the best-known spokesman abroad for Japan and Japanese business. He is the inventor of the Walkman – a craving for Beethoven apparently gave him the idea when he was playing golf – and has travelled extensively in Europe and North America. He knows his way around the corridors of Washington and London, as well as Tokyo itself. Small, wiry, silver-haired, he wears rimless spectacles, has a mischievous laugh, and spends his entire day explaining, planning and discussing on the move, with scarcely pause for breath. He works flat out all the time and loves it.

There is rarely a moment when he is not fiddling with some new device or demonstrating a portable compact disc player, tape recorder, miniature television or video camera which he just happens to have in his brief-case. When we travelled on the 'Bullet' train from Tokyo to Ngoya, he had at least two of these toys in his case and produced them for an enthusiastic demonstration on the platform. It is difficult to imagine the head of a British corporation selling his wares in Japanese to a visiting reporter at Paddington station – and obviously enjoying it.

Mr Morita's willingness to bare his soul, in public and in English, is rare among Japanese businessmen. Although he has a marked accent, his use of the language is always fluent and intelligible; if sometimes eccentric. To some of his senior compatriots, his lack of inhibition about voicing criticisms of western business methods may seem incautious and discourteous: he certainly does not conform to the broad tradition of the Japanese way of doing things and is far too westernised for their conservative tastes. Mr Morita ignores the criticism. He is, of course, westernised: he sent his sons to be educated in Britain, at Colchester, Atlantic College and the London School of Economics, and enjoys classical western music – he is a close friend of the conductor, Herbert von Karajan – but at the same time he is the personification abroad of the Japanese economic miracle.

When we were negotiating to meet him in Tokyo, we were told by telex that we did not need to worry about Mr Morita's ability to perform on television. 'Having been interviewed by BBC and other major TV stations in the world, Mr Morita knows very well how to respond in filming for a TV programme like yours' we were told. At one point in the negotiations, there was a hiccup in communications when we were told, with the utmost attention to courtesy and face-saving, that our request for some of Mr Morita's time was being turned down: it was only a question of lack of time, and 'not a reflection of any negative assessment of your programme'. Eventually, however, Mr Morita managed to squeeze us into his busy schedule to everyone's satisfaction.

Akio Morita was born in 1921, the eldest of three sons and the heir to the family business, which had for generations been the brewing of sake in a small factory at Ngoya. In his early years he developed an interest in electronics and liked to tinker with home-made radio sets. His father was eventually per-suaded that the second son would be a more suitable choice for the post of family brewery manager, and allowed Akio to go to Osaka Imperial University to study physics. After his gradua-tion from university in 1944, he was immediately commis-sioned as a lieutenant in the Imperial Navy. As a technical engineer with the Japanese Naval Research Centre, he was apparently working on a heat-seeking weapon when the war came to an abrupt end.

During his naval research work, he met Professor Masaru Ibuka, Chief Engineer of the Japan Precision Instrument Company. The two formed a partnership which lasted for more than forty years. In 1946, after a brief period of teaching at Tokyo University, they borrowed the equivalent of 500 US$ from the Morita family to set up a small electronics equipment manufacturing company. They called it the Tokyo Telecommunications Company: its Japanese name, Tokyo Tsushin Kogyo Kabushiki Kaisha, was impossible for most foreigners to pronounce, let alone remember, and it was later renamed Sony, which has roughly the same connotation and pronunciation in many languages. Mr Morita chose the name himself, he told me: it is based on the Latin word for sound, and made him and his colleagues feel as if they were a group of 'sunny boys' trying to get their company off the ground.

The sunny boys' first premises were in a bombed-out department store in the centre of Tokyo, but a year later they moved, with fifty employees, into former army barracks on the outskirts of the city. Success was at first elusive. The new company produced a batch of a hundred rice cookers, but the Japanese housewife was not impressed and not a single cooker was sold. A solitary example now has a place of honour in the company's museum in Tokyo. Their first tape recorder fared little better. A cumbersome and weighty affair, priced at about 500 US$, it used paper tape which they made from the output of a pulp mill: there was no plastic tape available in Japan at the time, Mr Morita explained. The tape recorders did not sell either, and the company was only saved from bankruptcy because Mr Morita managed to off-load the lot onto the Ministry of Education in a bulk contract for schools.

By then Ibuka and Morita had worked out a productive and stimulating relationship. Ibuka was the man who spotted all the best technical ideas, while Morita was salesman, negotiator, advertiser and spokesman. After its early fiascos, the company limped along for a couple of years with a few maintenence contracts from the Japanese Post Office and Broadcasting Company and made some vacuum tube voltmeters.

Then, in 1952, Ibuko's technical brilliance recognised that there was a future in the new transistor which had just been invented at Bell Laboratories in the United States. He and Morita bought the manufacturing rights from Western Electric, where some of the engineers had suggested that the new gadget might possibly have a use in a hearing aid, and started manufacturing the first portable transistor radio. The pitch of their advertising was that the radio was small enough to be carried about in a shirt pocket. Mr Morita told me that although this claim was not strictly true, he ensured that all the company's salesmen wore specially made shirts with slightly larger pockets than were usual – just big enough to take the new radios. Orders started to flow on a scale they had not previously thought possible.

The use of the transistor was the springboard for the launching of a whole new range of electronic products. The first AM transistor radio was produced in 1955, the first pocket-sized transistor radio and the first two-band transistor radio in 1957, the first FM transistor radio in 1958, an all-transistor television set in 1959, a transistorised video tape recorder in 1960 and the first small-screen transistorised television set in 1961.

While the new developments were pouring from Mr Ibuka's side of the business, Mr Morita was investigating marketing opportunities for Sony in Europe and North America. He first came to Britain in 1953, and in 1960 took his family to live in America, where they spent fifteen months in Manhattan while he was setting up the Sony Corporation of America. He joined a golf club and sent his sons to summer camp, and wrote a book criticising Japanese business attitudes. Its Japanese title was *Shinjitsuryokushigi* – 'The old school tie doesn't matter' – and it became a 1960s best seller in Tokyo. Mr Morita has subsequently flown backwards and forwards across the Pacific between Japan and America nearly 400 times.

While he was in New York, he commissioned an American advertising company to produce a series of low-key soft-sell advertisements for Sony products in which their country of origin was skilfully hidden. The aim was, he said, to teach potential customers about previously unknown, and therefore undesired, products. He is still sensitive about the attitude of other countries towards Sony and the Japanese name. When he visited the British stand at an international exhibition in Montreal in 1970, he told me, he noticed a television set on display in an elaborate tableau depicting what the average British family would be doing in the living room in the year 2000. A small piece of black tape had been carefully stuck over the manufacturer's name on the set: he sneaked up onto the stand and surreptitiously peeled it away. 'The nameplate was, of course, "Sony",' he said with an impish grin.

Sony is neither the biggest company in Japan, nor is it generally more successful than its competitors. But Mr Morita has established from scratch a world-wide reputation for his products, and no longer needs trick clothing to make them sell. The portable compact disc player, the Walkman, the 3.5 inch miniature floppy disc and the Video 8 camera, a miniature home video camera which could eventually replace 8mm home movies and current videos, have all helped to keep the company thriving. Overseas net sales in 1984, for instance, went up by more than sixteen per cent, and sales of video equipment by twelve and a half per cent.

The figures might have been even more impressive had the company not been so deeply committed to the Betamax video system, generally considered to be technically superior to its VHS rival. While Sony guarded its Betamax jealously, refusing to allow other companies to make it under licence, the originators of the VHS happily granted manufacturing licences to many other companies; they were therefore able to flood the market with their cheaper designs, which, although inferior, were more widely available and swept Sony's hopes before them. Mr Morita tried to put the most optimistic construction on the episode. Yes, he agreed, the VHS system had over-hauled Betamax, but he emphasised that Sony's separate system was still winning a significant share of the video market, although this was partly, as he admitted, because of the increasing general demand for videos.

Sony is not proud of the Betamax marketing failure. Privately officials admit that, with hindsight, their tactics might have been different. Meanwhile the Video 8 is a gamble the company cannot afford to lose. The Betamax will have to continue in production until the new technology can take over, but Mr Morita is, of course, confident that this will happen. He told me that he thought plastic records only had a life of a few more years, and that the compact disc and Video 8 would soon flood the market. Mr Morita's response may be somewhat predictable, but hearing it from Japan's super-salesman leaves a strong impression that his plausible view of the future is almost upon us.

I first met Mr Morita at the Sony headquarters in the Takanawa district of Tokyo. He had helped with the design of the building himself, but it was neither as large, nor as modern as I had expected. As I was conducted along a maze of corridors between different sections, I had the impression that various bits and pieces of the organisation had been hurriedly tacked on to the main block. Mr Morita's own office suite is cool and silent, with low-level lighting by discreet spotlights, viridian green wall-to-wall carpeting, a large nineteenth-century English clock, and displays of all the latest video devices and high-definition television screens. Visitors are conducted to a plain lounge where they are offered tea and have to sit on low modern settees arranged in a precise square around an equally low table.

Mr Morita is constantly attended by a couple of highly efficient young women secretaries: they have instant details of his engagements and, one suspects, considerable influence. As we tried to arrange a schedule for our filming, Mr Morita selected one of a row of sharp pencils in front of him and experimented with different permutations of the commitments in his diary, always relying on the assistance of his advisers. He tried several times to arrange his appointments in a certain way, but was forced to rub everything out and try again. It was a remarkably flexible procedure and not what we had imagined would happen in the office of a top Japanese executive.

The Japanese have a reputation abroad for fanatical dedication to work and organisation, but are not renowned for the sort of flexibility and instant decisions shown by the head of Sony. Perhaps we have misjudged them in the past, or perhaps Mr Morita is not typical: he certainly demonstrates some qualities which do not conform to the popular national image of the Japanese. He surrounds himself with bright young graduates, some of whom have no technical or scientific background, says that he is interested in new ideas wherever they come from, changes his mind, makes jokes, teases colleagues, and wants to explain Japan and his own business philosophy.

His refreshingly breezy approach allowed us to follow the maestro to a family ceremony at a Buddhist temple in his home village outside Ngoya. 'Japan is the only country in the world which has managed to unite modern technology with ancient tradition,' Mr Morita maintained. He arrived at the temple by Sony helicopter and chauffeur-driven car, and there was then a prolonged ritual bowing session as the members of his family party presented themselves before the priests. The temple is next door to the profitable sake brewery on which for several generations the Morita family fortunes depended, and has been endowed with profits from the consumer electronics business. The purpose of Mr Morita's visit to the temple was to honour the spirits of his ancestors, by annointing their graves with water ladled over the head stones to the chanting of monks. The most elaborate gravestone was an ornate marble affair which had been designed by Sony's Design Team. Not far away, there is also a new Morita family museum, an air-conditioned repository for thousands of historical documents recording the family's administration of their local estates over many generations.

Later that day, we saw Mr Morita again: he was on a panel of experts at a symposium on the decentralisation of industry, a sober affair in front of television cameras and a packed audience of Ngoya businessmen. The speeches droned on throughout the afternoon. Several of the audience appeared to have fallen asleep. I wondered whether they were under an obligation to attend, perhaps as a condition of promotion.

Moritas have held and still hold top positions in the firm, as Agnellis have done and probably always will do in Fiat. Ten per cent of Sony stock is owned by the Morita family. Mr Morita's late brother-law was for a time President of Sony, and his younger brother Massaki is Deputy President. In Sony, I was immediately struck by the wider Japanese business concept of 'family'. There were slogans around the offices proclaiming that although the tasks may not be easy, 'all members of the Sony family pull together to overcome difficulties, finding joy in creative work and pride in contributing their talents'.

When I asked Mr Morita what was meant by the Sony

family, he started by explaining the Japanese tradition of lifetime employment: 'Once we hire somebody, we cannot in practice fire him, so that means we have to keep our people together until they get to their retirement age of sixty years. So whatever happens we have to live together like a family.' He told me that the lifetime employment system meant that the company had to be particularly careful about the screening of new recruits, although there were, of course, occasional mistakes.

'We only have one life,' he said. Those who joined Sony were giving the company the brightest part of that life, and he therefore had an obligation to give them 'joy of life' through their work. If an employee was not as able as had been first thought, it was the company's responsibility to find him a position more suited to his abilities somewhere else in the company. In practice, he explained, it was almost impossible to fire anyone at Sony, which was why he had developed the concept of 'a sharing body like a family'.

It was as unthinkable for an employer to opt out of his responsibilities as for a parent to abandon his children: 'If you had some unlucky thing happening in your family, like a retarded child, for instance, the family still has to deal with him for the rest of his life. This means that if we find somebody who is not as capable as we expected, that is not his fault, but our fault for having selected him. Of course, if someone is really undesirable as a person we can fire him – if there is some very very serious problem – but otherwise we find some suitable job in which he can find some joy and will be motivated.'

I asked Mr Morita what would happen if he needed to make ten per cent of the workforce redundant, as has happened recently in some firms in Europe and North America. 'Because of that,' he said, 'we are very careful about increasing our numbers. Sometimes with the bad economic situation we find we have too many people, but if they are members of our family we have to keep them. The responsibility is on the management's side, so management is willing to sacrifice our profit to keep these people.'

When I put it to him that this was a very fine attitude as long as the economy was generally expanding, but might be more difficult in times of recession, he told me that in such a case he would have to find new businesses so that his people could be kept in employment: this was the Japanese custom. He quoted shipbuilding as an example. Japan is the world's largest shipbuilding country, but shipbuilding worldwide has gone down by fifty per cent. But no Japanese shipbuilder has gone bankrupt as a result, because all the companies affected by the recession found new businesses. One company for instance became the biggest manufacturer of oil rigs and drilling platforms, another had started making land-moving machinery, and there was even one Japanese shipbuilding company which had started a computer software company because it had so many computer software programmers. 'If we found our business was shrinking,' he said, 'naturally we must find new business in which we can give jobs. Because if you have a big family, even if the economy is bad, you have to do something and you must find jobs in order to survive.'

The image of the family is reinforced in many other ways in Sony's factories, where all employees, at whatever level, have to wear a company uniform: a beige nylon waistcoat trimmed with a purple line and carrying a name tag and pockets for pens. When I wondered whether the purpose of the uniform was to make everyone feel the same, Mr Morita told me that the idea had originated after the war when clothes were very expensive. The uniform had protected clothing which was then difficult and costly to replace. As the company expanded the uniform gradually became a tradition, although it was soon decided that its Mao style should be changed and a designer, Isi Miaki, was commissioned to produce a new look. Mr Morita thought that all Sony's employees were more comfortable wearing the jacket and felt at ease with the name tags and uniform.

At breakfast and lunchtime, all staff grades eat under the same roof in the Sony canteen; they pay for excellent meals with a plastic card which automatically deducts the charge from their salaries electronically. Another levelling influence is the company's fifteen-minute video news programme which is beamed from sets around the walls to the assembled diners. Every day the programme features weighty speeches and lectures about productivity, mingled with good news of the company's most recent successes.

For a western visitor there is perhaps a hint of Big Brother about the whole operation. I asked Mr Morita whether the video programme could be considered simply company propaganda, and whether he was trying to brainwash the people who worked for him. 'No, not really brainwashing purpose,' he replied, 'Naturally we need strong unity and we like everyone to have a strong sense of participation. Everyone should know more about the company and by doing this I think everybody feels that they are also participating in the company's policy. Some companies in the western world have employees who do not know where they are supposed to be going, and employees who cannot understand why their company has made a certain decision. We like to tell our people as much as we can about any important decision.'

It was almost a relief to notice that many of the employees in the canteen were not apparently keen to learn about the latest company decisions. They talked to their neighbours – just as they might in other countries one could think of – while the company news video on the wall above them continued earnestly congratulating itself.

Nevertheless, there is undoubtedly a strong sense of participation in Sony factories, just as there is in other factories in Japan. Sony has no dawn singing session of a company song, as I once saw at Matsushita Electric, but there are communal physical exercises and suggestion schemes with bonuses for the best ideas for improving productivity. Most impressive of all is the fact that on the production line there is no quality control department: the workers make all the necessary quality controls themselves. At the Betamax, Walkman and compact disc plants at Kisaruzu Iwane and Shiomi, about forty miles from Tokyo, all the assembly line workers are women and there is suprisingly little automation. We watched as rows of white gloved workers applied themselves with feverish concentration to the half finished models on the line in front of them. They neither talked to each other, nor paid the slightest attention to visitors.

The women work a shift from 8.10 am to 5.10 pm on an

alternating five and six day week. There is no union at the factories, but workers elect a committee which negotiates wages with the management and meets once a month. Twice a year, there are productivity bonus payments which amount to very significant sums, often the equivalent of about three months' pay. The plants are closed for nine days in the summer and nine in the winter, and workers are expected to take their holidays in these periods: extra days, although sometimes possible, are rarely taken. Maternity leave is three months with sixty per cent pay. In all sections of Sony it is common to find that workers are willing to stay behind for as much as two hours after the agreed finishing times. To leave earlier, I was told by one young westerner working for Sony, was to risk loss of face before one's contemporaries, who were showing a proud willingness to give the company more than the minimum. This is not apparently an isolated aberration of youthful enthusiasm, but a common phenomenon in all walks of Japanese business life.

I asked Mr Morita how he reacted to those abroad who claimed that the real reason for the success of Japanese business was the country's fanatical dedication to work, and the way his fellow countrymen often put their work before their private life, homes, even families. 'I think that whatever the criticism is, this is our policy and this is the way we must run,' he replied. He has little time for private life himself, and says that his business is also, in any case, his hobby.

He described how he saw his company as just like the crew of a ship. The ship, of course, was big and the crew large, but if one person made a mistake the whole ship might sink, and then everyone would be thrown into the water together. 'So we are all sharing the same fate,' he told me, 'if the ship gets into rough water or a storm, and if the water is coming in, no matter what kind of job or assignment the crew has, it is necessary for everyone to work together to save the whole ship, because in a crisis we must all work together.' He shrugged off the criticism of fanatical dedication to work by pointing out that in the west, managements often use the workers as 'a tool to make profit': 'We never regard our worker as a tool for profit; we are a family and we are sharing the same fate – so profit is important, but under the lifetime employment system everyone devotes their one life to the company, and I hope everyone then gets a real joy of life.'

If workers felt that they were forced to work just to earn money, how would they be motivated, he asked, because people were working for more than money. Management should try to give 'joy of work and joy of participation and the sense of participation to everyone'. During the war, for example, many people sacrificed their lives for their country: they were not seeking money, he said, but 'because of a real sense of mission they sacrificed their lives. So that means that if people are motivated with a real sense of mission, they should be encouraged.'

The strength of the electronics industry in Japan is the Japanese ability to organise production and marketing, rather than their achievements in original research. The British are generally recognised as a far more inventive collection of individuals, but never seem able to exploit what they invent. There are many examples, from the TSR2, hovercraft, high speed train and Sinclair scooter to the Triumph, BSA and Norton motorbikes, which all prove this sad rule. The Japanese were able to expoit their strengths in marketing and development many years ago, and their success was at first either not understood in the west, or was dismissed as something which could only have been achieved by unscrupulous tactics. For many years Japanese goods had a reputation for shoddiness – not always undeserved – and it was felt that they could only have been produced at their low price, so far from where they were sold, because they were cheap copies of other peoples' ideas churned out by a workforce which was dedicated to hard grind above all else.

Mr Morita made some pointed observations about this theory. I put it to him that Japanese success was the result, not of an ability to invent things, but of a skill in marketing and developing the inventions of others. He told me that he thought that after the war the Japanese realised that they were far behind in technology and so agreed to learn as fast as they could. They had to take ideas at first from outside, but then applied what they had learned to their own creative skills.

Although he admitted that in the past people overseas had said that what the Japanese did was steal ideas and supply, develop, and distribute what others had thought of first, he insisted that there had been great changes in the last decade: 'We have changed incredibly, particularly in production engineering. We can now make a very reliable and high-quality product, and we have also created many new products in the world.

Mr Morita and many other Japanese feel that they have not been given credit for their particular skills at actually making an idea work in practice. In Europe, he told me, there were many who felt very pleased with themselves for having an idea: 'Anyone can have an idea, but in industry very few people make that idea into real industry.' An idea by itself is not worth anything, he pointed out: 'Our idea is to utilise a good idea from anybody – also from us – and use this idea to make something in a real industry.'

He thought that the secret of the Japanese success in utilising ideas lay in their production engineering: 'You know, in the western world – if I criticise – you appreciate the scientist, sometimes you don't appreciate the engineer.' The work of the scientist was, he agreed, very important in developing a new concept or new invention, but without the engineer the idea could not be utilised by the general public. 'So the secret of Japanese industry,' he declared, 'is simply that we have worked very hard to make a new idea into a real and useful product.'

While they find it difficult to accept the lack of recognition from outsiders for their production achievements, the Japanese are also still sensitive about charges of plagiarism. At Sony's headquarters in Tokyo I visited a vast exhibition of the latest electronic devices produced by the firm called 'Media World'. It was open only to the firm's guests and clients, and included examples of electronic technology which were obviously so specialised that they would find no place in the domestic marketplace. There was, for instance, a device which could superimpose a new hairstyle on a subject who was sitting in front of a television camera; the result could be printed out instantly at the side of the machine. There were other devices which could print huge enlargements from any television screen, as well as special high-definition television screens, robot-stacking devices for video libraries, and a roof-top robot television camera which could be remotely controlled and zoomed into any hotel or office window within sight (which might, I felt, contravene bye-laws about the protection of privacy). Some of the equipment on display at 'Media World' looked remarkably similar to inventions which can be seen in the United States or Europe. Sony's new office computer, for example, was not unlike the Apple Macintosh, and the compact disc players, of which the company is so proud, were originally developed by Phillips in Europe.

Mr Morita, quick to defend himself against the charge that the Japanese simply take ideas from others, lays great emphasis on the way his company has developed the compact disc in partnership with Phillips, and told us that the way the two companies had shared the development of digitalised sound recording technology was a good example of how a Japanese and a western company could combine to produce something new. 'I think such a kind of co-operation will be a new type of international co-operation,' he suggested. But he admitted that another motive was the 'enormous costs' of developing advanced technology at the moment, and predicts that the next stage will be the co-operation of perhaps three different companies for the international exchange of technical ideas. This would, he said, produce dramatic savings in costs.

Unlike Fiat, which relies for its success on selling seventy per cent of its output to the Italian home market, Sony sells less than a third of what it produces in Japan. Seventy per cent of the company's sales are abroad, and almost half its shares are also sold overseas. The Japanese have been so successful at making and selling domestic electronic goods that they have virtually swamped the market in North America. In Times Square in New York, most of the gaudy neon advertising displays feature Japanese names, Sony's included, which were almost unknown in the United States little more than a decade ago. The message is, of course, repeated all over America, Europe and much of the rest of the world. Japan's marketing success has had a catastrophic effect on comparable industries in the United States, where there have been passionate debates about sanctions and protectionism.

Mr Morita believes that protectionism 'is not the right way in this free economic system'. If one side went the protectionist way and protectionism spread, he told me, the whole economy would shrink, and with the increase in world population and in international demand the 'shrinking way' could not be good: 'We must expand our economy and industrial work.' I asked him how Japan could satisfy Washington that obstacles would not be put in the way of American exports to Japan, as had happened in the past. 'We cannot force our people to buy an American product,' he said, 'and we cannot force the Americans to buy Japanese. We never force the Americans to buy; they choose our product. Now American industry is buying from Japan. Why? – because the price is right.' He disagreed that there had been huge barriers in the past to the attempts of foreign firms to export to Japan, and claimed that as far as the Japanese consumer electronics industry was concerned there never had been any barrier. Instead he accused foreign firms of having never bothered to investigate the market in Japan as the Japanese themselves had done in other countries.

Sony is one of a number of Japanese companies which anticipated marketing difficulties some time ago and started making plans to set up subsidiaries abroad. In the late 1950s, Sony made a definite decision about entering the world market. 'After the war the economy was fractured, so if we depend only on the Japanese market, then when the economy is good we make good business, and if the economy goes down we have difficulty,' he told me. 'We knew we could find customers who wanted to buy our products anywhere in the world. So that is why we started to market our products worldwide and why I have been travelling all over the world since the late fifties. I came to England in the fifties. I knew England would be a very very important market for us, so that is why we set up Sony UK.' Mr Morita has paid annual visits to Britain since 1953.

In 1970, he met Prince Charles at an Expo reception in Osaka. He told me that Prince Charles suggested that if Sony ever thought of opening a factory in Britain, they should consider siting it in Wales. Two years later Sony did indeed decide to open a Trinitron TV factory at Bridgend in South Wales, although not perhaps as a direct result of royal lobbying: Prince Charles opened it in 1974. In 1982, when Sony opened an extension to the factory, he dispatched his wife to the ceremony. The Princess, wearing a Sony cap and pursued by photographers, was shown over the plant, and at the end of the ceremony was rewarded by Mr Morita with the presentation of a matching pair of his-and-hers Walkmans in a velvet case emblazoned with the Prince's coat of arms. Mr Morita has little to learn about public relations.

For the first ten years, he told me, Sony UK did not make a profit, but he had enough confidence in the eventual importance of the market to continue with long-term investment plans which eventually started to produce results. Long-term planning is characteristic of many Japanese foreign ventures in industry. He claimed that he was very satisfied with the quality of the Sony workforce in Britain, but admitted that he had felt it necessary to import some of the Japanese concepts of personnel management to Wales, and had tried to persuade the initial management group that the workers at the Welsh factory should be treated not as tools for profit, but as partners in the whole operation. Whenever he visited the factory, he said, he had lunch with the workers in the single cafeteria and tried to meet as many of them as he could. He made sure that management always went through the production line, and that workers and managers were close to each other.

Sony's workers in Wales, who have been interviewed several times on television, seem to approve of the new style of management. By 1983, Sony had a thousand employees in the UK, producing 180,000 television sets a year in a factory where the entire workforce, including management, turns up for work at 7.30 am, wears identical Sony jackets, and eats family-style at round tables in a single canteen. When the workers leave at 4.00 pm every afternoon, in a fleet of buses and cars, the managers and engineers stay on for at least another two hours and often considerably longer, just as they do in Sony factories in Japan: it is not compulsory, but it is expected.

The Japanese family approach to business was imported to Wales alongside careful tuition about mutual responsibility and the duty to achieve the highest possible standards: life-long employment is guaranteed, as it is in Japan, and there have, perhaps not surprisingly, been no strikes. Although workers may belong to any union, negotiations are conducted only with one. As well as providing long-term employment, Sony UK has entered enthusiastically into sponsorship of local social activities, and in 1985 ran a national competition to discover a new up-and-coming rock'n'roll band.

As Mr Morita apparently does not think that there is much wrong with the British as workers, I asked him who was to blame for the general industrial decline in Britain. 'I think that management must change attitude, if I say frankly; that's my opinion,' he declared. Once again, he emphasised that his philosophy was based on the principle that all employees at all levels were sharing the same fate in their organisation, and that the management should therefore treat all workers as partners. When I asked him what British management could do in practice to improve the lot of industry, he was careful not to offend with any too specific advice. The engineer should be more appreciated because companies like Sony need engineering to make a good product, he told me, but the engineer must in turn also appreciate the workforce: 'Without really good co-operation in the workforce, we cannot produce a good product. So if in the company everyone admires one another, admires his job and is responsible to the others, you can get much stronger unity in the company.'

When I asked him to be more specific about how British management might be able to bring about such a happy state of affairs, Mr Morita gave me the answer he had once given an American friend: 'Whenever I visit our branch office or one of our factories, I try to speak to all the workers about what we are trying to do, and try to explain our company policy to make everybody feel they are members of the same company.' The American friend apparently took his advice to heart: whenever he subsequently went on a visit to any of his companies he gathered all the people together and spoke very frankly to them about his intentions. A few years later, Mr Morita said,

'He told me that the suggestion had worked very well.' The primary problem in modern industry is, he maintains, communication between management and workforce: 'If you did not know your management how could you trust him?' Even if it is not possible in a big factory for the manager to know everyone, Mr Morita says he should try to meet as many as possible and at least show his face to everybody.

A natural and cautious diplomat, Mr Morita was careful to point out that he did not think of himself as an adviser to British industry, and felt that without any really deep knowledge it would be dangerous to make suggestions. He laughed when I invited him to speculate about why it was that the British seemed so good at inventing things and no good at all at putting them into the market place, and without directly criticising British industrial attitudes spoke again about what happened in Sony: 'The production line is very important, and in our own case we have many graduate engineers working in the factories. We also encourage each worker to suggest good ideas to improve his or her work and to improve quality and reliability.' In February 1983, the Bridgend Ideas Group, known within Sony UK as BIG, even sent three girls from the factory in Wales to tell a Sony meeting in Tokyo about their own ideas for improving production.

I asked *how* a manager could encourage the workforce to feel the required depth of involvement with the company. Mr Morita replied that the management must first make each worker understand his or her responsibility, and admitted that at Sony a great deal of time was spent teaching workers their duties: 'The worker must understand what will happen to the final product if someone, for example, forgot to solder some small part. On a colour television set it might mean that the final picture had some fault.' Each worker on the production line should know how important his or her job was to the final product, and he was convinced that 'If such a responsibility is taught, the workers soon feel that responsibility themselves.' The atmosphere inside a factory was, in his opinion, also very important, but it could, he repeated, be improved if everyone had a sense of participation, because then people could get 'joy out of their participation' in the work: 'Anybody likes to enjoy life and likes to have some satisfaction in their job, so management should try everything to give joy in that participation and some feeling of responsibility.' Money was not, he believed, an adequate motivation.

Like Sir John Harvey-Jones of ICI, Mr Morita thinks that marketing is one area in which British industry has fallen short. Marketing is not just selling, he maintains, because when something new comes out the public does not at first know how to utilise it. 'We must educate our customers,' he told me. 'In Japan we don't have anything and we must import everything. So to acquire money we must sell our products worldwide. That's why we started thinking of how we could sell our products, especially, in our own case, because we are always creating new products. We found that it was important to educate the market.'

It was because he did not think that it was possible to educate the market effectively through a third party that he decided Sony should open its own marketing organisations abroad. 'My original job was running all over the world to educate our own sales force in what meaning their product had for the general public,' he told me, 'My job was how to convince people.' How did he go about educating the market, I asked. Advertising was important, naturally, he said, but also educating salesmen and dealers. He gave the example of the introduction of video recorders. At first no one thought that the VCR could be important or useful in the home. The biggest disadvantage of television, however, was that unless the audience was sitting in front of it, all its information would be wasted, whereas a newspaper could be put aside and read later: 'I pointed out that with the video recorder, you could change the nature of television. It was a fast facility to grab information in your hand, so while you are away you can record a programme on a video cassette at your home.' This, he said, was the sort of message which had to be passed on to the public – in other words, marketing.

In 1976, his enthusiasm for VCRs came up against a problem when Universal Studios and Walt Disney Productions took the Sony Corporation of America to court, claiming that the manufacture and sale of the Betamax VCRs constituted an infringement of the copyright laws in America. The Supreme Court ruled in 1984 that using a video recorder at home was a fair use and decided in favour of Sony: the company's sales did not, after all, make the company liable for any copyright infringement of the recorded material. As Sony's Betamax programme was beginning to run into difficulties, those in charge of the sales' drive must have been relieved that an annoying distraction had disappeared.

I asked Mr Morita if the British were good at salesmanship or whether he thought they found the idea of selling somehow disreputable. Without, of course, implying criticism, he said that in the old days some British companies had believed in the old concept that if the product was right, people would come to buy. In the new technological world, with new products coming out 'neck and neck', no company could wait until the customer came forward. 'We must tell our customer why he needs this new product,' he said again, 'such educational work is the key to marketing. It is the new concept.' Some British companies might still be old-fashioned in this, he thought, but this did not mean that the attitude of all firms in Britain was backward.

Sony's own sales' charts have not always shown a continuous upward trend. In 1983, the company ran into difficulties mainly because of the disastrous slump in Betamax sales, which slipped for the first time in eight years, and profits fell for the second consecutive year. Zenith, Toshiba and NEC abandoned Sony's Beta system and chose the VHS produced by Sony's archrival, Matsushita Electric. Sony's share of the VCR market fell from sixty-two per cent in 1977 to twenty-five per cent by the beginning of 1984. The company was also having difficulties with its Mavica camera, which had been launched with noisy fanfares but was not exactly plentiful in the shops – there had been disputes about standards – and sales of the new SMC 70 personal computer were disappointing.

Mr Morita was blamed by some industrial commentators for allowing Sony to become eclipsed in the race for new technology and for being over-confident. In any event the company was forced, like other companies in other countries, to make some major changes in order to survive. There was a freeze on recruitment, bonuses for top executives were cut for the first time, more money was spent on research and development, investment in new plant and equipment was cut back, and there were economies imposed at all levels. It was, said his critics, all too obvious that Mr Morita had never had any formal management training. During his company's least successful period, Sony's usually ebullient chairman occasionally refused to talk to reporters: he was tired of reading about Sony's problems, he said, and would talk only when there was something good to say.

The crisis came to a head during Sony's 1984 AGM, which lasted for more than thirteen hours, a length previously unheard of in Japanese business history, and was attended by 400 shareholders. The length of the meeting was attributed in part to new laws preventing the traditional Japanese 'Sokiya' system under which firms entered into financial agreements with token shareholders (the Sokiya), who in the past had been guaranteed to agree with any suggestions and not to ask awkward questions. In 1984 Sony shareholders had good reason to ask questions to which it was difficult to find satisfactory answers. Many of those at the meeting were understandably worried about their investments: Sony had shown a thirty-five per cent drop in net profits over a year.

Fortunately it was soon obvious that demand had begun to pick up again and Sony's new hopes, the portable compact disc player, the Video 8 camera, the new high-definition screens and a new technique for data storage using lasers to read video discs all helped to restore confidence. Mr Morita's predictions that all would be well, which he had optimistically continued to make throughout the period of sliding sales, seemed to have been vindicated. The only doubts remaining were concerned with the company's continuing vulnerability in relying so heavily on the consumer electronic market, where spending might suddenly slow down with little warning. At the moment Sony is about an eighty per cent consumer and twenty per cent non-consumer company. Its plan is to level out the imbalance by the 1990s, but this, of course, will depend on how successful it is in the new areas of office electronics, and compact disc and data technology.

Not far from Sony's headquarters in Tokyo, Mr Morito lives in splendid style in a palatial modern house which is reputed to have cost half a million pounds and is lined with the latest of his firm's gadgetry. He and his wife, Yoshiko, designed the decor together: they wanted the best available international style, including imported Tiffany china and Italian silver. A variety of hi-fi speakers with exhausting levels fill the house with western classical music. There is a meticulously restored pianola with a repertoire of 200 rare piano rolls and, in the basement, an underground swimming pool.

Unlike many Japanese businessmen, Mr Morita has not made a habit of entertaining guests in clubs and bars each evening. He is either holding late meetings at his offices, or entertaining people at home, western-style, with his wife. In spite of the long-standing connections with sake through the family's brewery business, he does not drink. Mrs Morita, who has been involved in such company activities as the design of the uniform worn by Sony girls, is not considered a typical Japanese wife, and has been called intelligent and forceful, qualities which have no doubt been useful in her career as a journalist writing for glossy magazines. Mr Morita is an excellent and obviously fit sportsman: his only relaxation appears to be a regular tennis game with colleagues at a local sports' club (he usually manages to beat them convincingly) or a game of golf, almost a compulsory occupation for Japanese businessmen, often accompanied by his wife.

He is instantly recognisable everywhere, with his silvery hair, parted straight down the middle, and his firm, straight-forward and most un-Japanese handshake. Some of his countrymen apparently suspect him of being if not un-Japanese, then at best suspiciously maverick. Certainly he appears perfectly at ease as he flits between east and west, between Tokyo, London and New York. He is, without doubt, the best-known Japanese businessman in the world, and through all his travelling over more than thirty years has felt naturally at ease wherever he has tried to further Sony's cause.

It is a cause as dear to his heart as ICI is to Sir John

Harvey-Jones, or the inherited empire of Fiat to Giovanni Agnelli, or ARCO to its creator Robert Anderson. It is, however, difficult to imagine quite the same sense of family commitment to a firm, even one which has been rescued, inherited, or created by a European or American industrialist, as Mr Morita feels to Sony. He is always happy to talk about his vast extended family, the firm which he established and its creations, which are all too familiar to competitors in the high streets of Europe and America. It is sometimes difficult, however, while admiring his indefatigable salesmanship, his admirable command of English and his ability to sell to the English-speaking world, not to be reminded of Mr Agnelli's warnings of Trojan horses and Sir John Harvey-Jones' hope that 'Super Tosh' of Toshiba may help western industry to understand and capitalise on the unfamiliar attitudes of Japan. Nevertheless Akio Morita has, more than any other business-man, bridged the cultural and industrial gap between east and west.

STANLEY HO OF HONG KONG & MACAO

CHAPTER 5

BETTING ON A CERTAINTY

In the bustling streets of Hong Kong and Kowloon, and in the steaming alleyways of the Portuguese colony of Macao forty miles to the west, no name is better known than that of Stanley Ho, multi-millionaire businessman, Latin-American ballroom dancing enthusiast, shipping magnate, jet-foil visionary, importer and exporter, patron of the RAF Museum at Hendon, and operator of a vast and lucrative chain of international casinos. He is less well known outside the Far East, and in any case seems to prefer anonymity wherever possible. He is a quiet, shy, enigmatic man who has so much money that he says he does not know how rich he really is: the figure is changing all the time and the calculations would be too complicated.

Stanley Ho has spent most of his life profiting from the Chinese passion for any game of chance. In doing so he has built himself a financial empire which has been constantly expanding for more than forty years. 'When times are bad,' he told me in the back seat of his third Rolls Royce, 'the Chinese gamble, but the odd thing is that when times are good the Chinese also gamble – so I win both ways.' Mr Ho also runs casinos in Spain, Portugal, Australia and the Phillipines, but the biggest and most lucrative section of his business empire is in the Portuguese colony of Macao, where in addition to casinos he owns several major hotels and most of the ferries.

Every year more than three million Hong Kong Chinese make the ferry journey from Hong Kong to Macao simply to gamble in one of Stanley Ho's casinos; most of them travel in one of Mr Ho's ferries and stay in one of his hotels. The establishments they patronise not only benefit Mr Ho's own coffers, they also contribute more than 600 million Hong Kong dollars every year to the local economy. Recently Mr Ho has started to branch out from purely gambling enterprises and is spending more of his incalculable riches on other businesses. He buys, builds and manages blocks of apartments and offices in Hong Kong, and has built one of the colony's four stock exchanges. He also runs import and export companies in some profusion; but apparently still not satisfied he has now gone even further.

In 1985 he unveiled the Shun Tak Centre, $2000 million worth of luxury office and hotel accommodation in a scarlet steel skeletal construction which dominates the Hong Kong waterfront. On the top the penthouse suite overlooks the entire harbour: it is now Mr Ho's own office, and from it he also has an excellent view of the main jetfoil ferry terminal through which all his customers have to pass before they reach the Macao section of his operation. Of course, he owns the jetfoils as well. As Stanley Ho told us, he wins both ways. In the gambling business he is, one could say, betting on a certainty.

Born in Hong Kong in 1921, with a Chinese father and a Portuguese mother, Stanley Ho was regarded as something of an outsider by both Chinese and European societies, and was determined at an early age that he would one day be recognised as a success. When the Japanese invaded Hong Kong in 1941, he was a student at Hong Kong University. After eight days, the Hong Kong government surrendered and many of his uncles and cousins, he told me, were interned. He was more fortunate: he had been working in the air raid wardens' office, and managed to take off his uniform and run away and hide. He was smuggled out of Hong Kong and offered a job as a junior secretary in Macao in the Macao Co-operative Company by a Chinese friend of his father. The young Stanley Ho could not have found anywhere more suited to his talents than the fevered atmosphere of Macao in those days.

Macao is tiny, a small promontory linked by a narrow causeway to the islands of Taipa and Coloane on the west bank of the Pearl River. Its total area is barely 16 square kilometres, with a population of half a million. Macao has been Portuguese since it was set up in 1557 as a trading post with China, and has existed for hundreds of years as a strange geographical anomaly, harbouring a rich mixture of entrepeneurs, exiles and eccentrics and making its living from anything which comes to hand. The tea which was ditched in Boston harbour in 1773 was part of a consignment from Macao, which has, over the years, dealt in tea, cloth, spices and opium. In 1941 the colony was under Portuguese control and neutral. Thousands of refugees from Hong Kong mingled with a variety of other nationalities there and food shortages were chronic. For those who had negotiating skills, languages, a capacity for hard work and the right connections, many lucrative opportunities for trade arose.

A few years before Stanley Ho fled to Macao, his father had been declared bankrupt – in Chinese society such a thing was a disgrace to the entire family – and had run away, I was told, and the family had become very poor. His mother became ill with tuberculosis, pawned all her jewellery and auctioned the family properties one by one. On her death bed, she made her son promise that he would redeem the family's name, purge the disgrace of financial ruin and, if possible, make himself a millionaire. He promised to do his best. He was nineteen when he stepped off the boat in Macao: he was single and single-minded, and knew that he had all the right qualifications for making a fortune.

The company Stanley Ho first joined had several functions. It represented the Portuguese, the Chinese and the interests of the Japanese military, and had been set up to arrange barter deals between the Macao government and the Japanese authorities. The young Stanley learned Japanese and started work early each morning, staying in his office until last thing at night. His job was to send flour, beans, rice and sugar – all collected from the Japanese and from Canton – to the government warehouses. In return he received surplus equipment from the government, 'like generators, tug boats, launches and so forth'. 'It was very interesting work,' Mr Ho told me, 'but at the same time a very tense situation. Every day in Macao there were murders, and it was very interesting that whenever you had a party at Government House, you could see the British Consul or the Japanese Consul racing to shake hands with the Governors first. It was at the same time a paradise in the Far East, because with Portugal being neutral, we in Macau could enjoy having almost everything you needed, provided you had money.'

In those days, Mr Ho said, it was possible to make a million dollars a week. One is left with the strong impression that he very often did, and that no one who had not lived in Macao through those heady days would ever really understand how. I asked him to explain how it had been possible for him to make so much money so quickly. 'Well, you see, daily necessities, they go up very fast, the prices climb very fast,' he explained in his quiet, inscrutable and charming manner. 'I have connections with government, sometimes we are given opportunities to buy the surplus from the government and then we have a chance to make quite a lot of money.'

Other people, of course, had exactly the same sort of opportunities, so how was it that he had been able to beat them? 'All very true,' Mr Ho agreed in honeyed tones, 'but through hard work, because you had to follow the market very closely and then you had to work very fast, because competition was so keen you could lose it in a couple of hours. I was single, I worked very hard and I managed to learn Japanese in six months. A lot of opportunities came from the Japanese, because they had many of the commodities. Apart from the normal supplies they gave to the government, they had lots of surplus and they sold to the outside market.' The Japanese, we were told, were interested in certain commodities which they were willing to barter with cotton yarn, foodstuffs and all the other things which were much needed and which were very expensive.

What turned Mr Ho from a hard-working and successful entrepeneur into a multi-million phenomenon was a single ability: his skill in exploiting the Chinese passion for gambling. In Hong Kong after the war, the only place where a gambler could bet openly was – and still is – at so-called Happy Valley, the home of the Royal Hong Kong Jockey Club. A prestigious institution which has just celebrated its centenary, it dominates the colony's social life and contributes a significant sum every year to a variety of charities and welfare projects. Its stands are overflowing with eager spectators of every kind, while in the tiers of sumptuous offices and club rooms above there are opportunities for business deals to be discussed; the participants are attended by unobtrusive waiters and the progress of the racing below can be observed through spectacular windows which overlook the sprawling city from a commanding position.

It is difficult to comprehend the extent of the wealth which the Royal Hong Kong Jockey Club absorbs and disperses. General Sir John Archer, its main spokesman, told me that there was an 'immense propensity for betting among the Chinese in Hong Kong'. The club, he claimed, generated the highest average racing turnover anywhere in the world. The government took ten and a half per cent of the total, and Sir John told me: 'When you put it all together at the end of the year, and you add things like corporation tax, profits tax, entertainment tax, then we actually contributed to the government something like 2.8 billion dollars last year . . . about eight per cent of the Government's revenue.' He explained that the Club took seven per cent of the turnover to pay its 12,000 staff and to finance the racing itself: 'Everything below the line we transfer to a charities' company, and we give that money away to charity.' The stewards distribute it to a variety of projects ranging from small gifts to projects in the 400 to 500 million dollar range.

In the early 1960s, when Stanley Ho had established his trading empire in Macao, he began to look around for new opportunities. 'I could not agree that Hong Kong should enjoy all the prosperity while Macao in 1962 was like a dying city,' he told me. 'After all, we are two little tiny places left in South East Asia where you can still enjoy freedom of speech and thought, and so why should one place prosper so much while Macao was going downhill?' At the time, there was a small gambling operation in Macao which earned a modest revenue for the colonial government.

When the tender was announced for the new Macao gambling franchise, Mr Ho saw an opportunity: 'I knew that gambling could be used as a subsidy in the development of tourism. All Macao needed was tourism to bring it nearer to Hong Kong. You needed a lot of money to buy fast hydrofoils and ferries. In order to promote Macao to become more prosperous, the first objective was transportation – I must have faster boats between Hong Kong and Macao. The second was that I must build more decent hotels, because in those days there was not one single decent hotel in Macao, and the third thing was that I needed to get more tourists into Macao.'

In bidding for the Macao gambling franchise, Mr Ho was already in a strong position. He had an intimate knowledge of the local business community and of how certain strings had to be pulled, and was completely at home in both the Chinese and Portuguese languages and cultures. He had already amassed a significant amount of capital, knew how to borrow more on the most favourable rates, and, perhaps most important of all, had a steely resolve to win and a capacity to take risks with bold ideas.

When I asked him how he, as the head of a private company, had managed to win the gambling franchise, he explained that he had been able to offer the government many more benefits than his competitors. 'It wasn't easy, it was a hard fight,' he admitted, 'We offered to open up a new channel in the outer harbour. In those days, the old harbour was completely silted up. If you wanted to go to Macao, there were no day trips, so you had to spend the night in Macao. And you must take the slow boat to China – those ferries taking four hours and having to go all the way into the inner harbour.' 'A lot of people said "Stanley Ho is a pirate," ' he told me, ' "He promises, but all those dreams will never come true." But I have proved to them that everything I've promised has worked. I succeeded in opening the channel by dredging. They said it would be silted up within a week – it is still going on in good order.'

He admitted, however, that in spite of the glowing promises and development plans, it had been a hard struggle to beat his competitors: 'It took me six trips to Lisbon, and it was a long-drawn battle.' When I asked why it had been so difficult, he explained that the opposition had tried to stop all the existing boats: they hoped to force him to bring his customers from Hong Kong by junk, which would have made the whole project unviable. But even such tactics were more gentlemanly than some of the techniques apparently used by the old concessionaires.

'It was a very, very dirty fight,' Mr Ho told me, 'They even tried to scare me and said they might take my life. But I called all their bluffs.' He refused to be drawn about how the threats had been made or countered, but I was left with the impression that the phrase 'dirty fight' does less than justice to the full story of the struggle for Macao's gambling prize. Mr Ho insists that he won the franchise simply by offering the government more inducements than his opponents: apart from dredging the harbour, he was also responsible for clearing the waterfront of a vast shanty town and rehousing 900 families who were sheltering there. 'It was a social problem, and it was very difficult to clear them,' he told me. The bulldozing of the hovels and rehousing of their occupants at the same time enabled Mr Ho's company to take control of many acres of valuable development land.

As his first priority, Stanley Ho, the managing director of the newly formed company STDM – Sociedade de Turismo e Diversoes de Macao – decided that he would have to invest in a vastly improved ferry service. If the new corporation was to be at all profitable, gamblers would have to be brought from Hong Kong in droves. The gambling franchise was to run for twenty-five years until 1987, but STDM had to pay an increasing share of profits to the Macao government on a sliding scale. The company brought the first hydrofoil service to the Far East, and eventually the first jetfoil service. Mr Ho also embarked on an energetic building programme in Macao. Over the next twenty years, STDM built three hotels and five casinos, two of them open twenty-four hours a day.

The original franchise was won by a consortium of four businessmen, led by Stanley Ho, who was the new managing director but shared the financial arrangements with Teddy Yip, Cheong Yiu Teng and Henry Fok. Henry Fok was a Hong Kong property millionaire who many years later was coopted by the mainland Chinese to help draft the new Hong Kong constitution. Stanley Ho also had close links with mainland China, and often crossed the border to spend his scarce leisure time on duck-shooting expeditions in the neighbouring province of

Guandong. He later initiated feasibility studies with Lufthansa in China's Zuhai 'Special Economic Zone' for an international airport which it was thought would serve Macao from China.

When the four men first combined, they were still far from having earned such honoured places in the capitalist establishment, and there were occasional glimpses of some of the initial strains under which their company struggled. We had heard, for instance, that in the early years there was some kind of disagreement between Stanley Ho and another partner called Yip Hon. When I asked Mr Ho to explain the background to the dispute, I gained the impression that under the smooth and placid exterior of STDM's public pronouncements there had been volcanic forces at work

Yip Hon had been a professional gambler, who 'thought he knew more than everybody else' and had been brought into STDM because Mr Ho knew nothing about gambling himself and needed help and advice. Mr Hon was 'very old fashioned', I was told, 'He did not believe in improvements. He refused to introduce American or European games into the casinos. He wanted to carry on the old way. They had been operating the casinos with croupiers in singlets and slippers. No-one could speak a word of English. All the games were Chinese.'

In addition to this disagreement about reforming the casinos, Mr Ho came to feel that Yip Hon knew nothing about administration or organisation. There was only one solution: 'We bought him out for 300 million dollars,' Mr Ho told me. 'His original investment was 50,000 dollars. I think he should be satisfied with 300 million. We are anyway.' They are still friends, Mr Ho maintains, and often sit at the same table at functions, but he does not think that Yip Hon would have much of a chance if he tried to win the gambling franchise himself when it next came up for renewal: 'I think he's become much too old. He's over eighty and in another seven years time, who knows where he will be. No chance.'

At the time of our interview, Yip Hon was thought to be somewhere in the United States on business: we understand he has interests in Las Vegas, as well as owning the Trotting Track in Macao. Later, in a statement issued by his lawyers, he claimed that Mr Ho's account of their separation was completely untrue, but he neither elaborated nor offered an alternative version of events.

I asked Stanley Ho whether he thought STDM would win the gambling franchise next time. In his most polished and noncommittal manner, which still could not disguise a strange glitter in his eyes, he said that he did not really know because he was getting old himself: 'In seven years time I don't know whether I'd like to retire, but – as a man who likes to work so much, I don't know. I'm in love with working. I think I would like to bid for it. I have very seldom lost in my life. I've been very lucky so far – and I'm a fighter.'

His ability to concentrate his energies on the task of making money soon started to earn its rewards, and through-out the 1970s his business empire steadily expanded. In Hong Kong, he started to buy property companies and built or managed blocks of flats and offices. He was so successful that he was eventually appointed President of the Real Estate Developers' Association of Hong Kong. He became a major shareholder in the Cathay Pacific airline and at the picturesque suburb of Aberdeen in Hong Kong set up the world's biggest floating Chinese restaurant. A vast and ornate construction, it is covered with intricate carvings and gaudily painted panelling on four stories – fortunately it seems to be at permanent anchor and rarely has to go anywhere. It was followed by the purchase of the Shatin, a second floating restaurant, and more recently the Tower Club of Kowloon, an exclusive private club linked to an association of 170 others scattered across America and the Far East, and catering to the leisure needs of the exclusive minority, the only people in a position to afford its prices.

During this period Mr Ho was eager to start investing overseas, and in the mid-1970s he set up the West Point Casino in Tasmania and won a gambling franchise at Dili in Portu-guese Timor. He also bought gambling enterprises in the Phillipines and Malaysia. But some of his investment decisions were not as lucrative as others. In 1975, for instance, he bought a large piece of land from the Shah of Iran and spent more than twenty million US dollars building a racecourse in Teheran itself. The operation was ready just in time for the Revolution and has not earned a penny since. 'One has to be patient,' Mr

Ho said. He told me that he had the horse-racing franchise in Iran for twenty-five years: 'One never knows how one's luck may go.'

One of his more successful ventures has been to buy into gambling businesses in Spain and Portugal. He spent over $43 million on buying land plus a quarter of the total shares of the casino at Murcia on the coast of south east Spain, and was quoted in the local papers as saying he would have liked to invest more if the law about what proportion of a business could be owned by a foreigner were relaxed. The casino had to pay a fifty per cent tax to the Spanish government, perhaps an indication of the potential profits of such an operation.

Meanwhile Mr Ho and STDM managed to persuade the Governor of Macao, Rear Admiral Vasco Almeida e Costa, to renegotiate the casino franchise there and extend it until 1991. Mr Ho is reported to have accepted 'with pleasure' the stringent new conditions which were imposed in the agreement. These included the payment of 200 million patacas to the government – about 30 million US dollars – and 500 million Hong Kong dollars as a franchise tax. STDM was also obliged to pay for the rehousing of 2000 families, and to pay a twenty-five per cent tax on the annual gambling turnover, to be increased by one per cent every year until it reached thirty per cent. It is no wonder that the local economy received a boost from the new source of wealth. In 1981, for example, Macao's exports of textiles, electronics and toys increased by forty-six per cent, and between 1978 and 1981 the colony's balance of payments surplus doubled.

The source of all this wealth is, of course, the gambling passion of the Chinese in Hong Kong, next door to Macao. Every year several million of them make the jetfoil journey from the Shun Tak Centre ferry terminal, staring through portholes at the passing junks and cargo vessels as their huge craft roar across the muddy waters of the South China Sea on a forty-five minute journey. A few passengers, of course, are travelling for reasons not necessarily connected with gambling, but the vast majority file off the ferries and immediately make their way to one of Mr Ho's casinos.

The biggest, most famous and most popular of these is the

Hotel Lisboa, with rooms for 1000 gamblers in 450 suites. Its architecture is in a style which is difficult to describe, a sort of Blackpool wedding-cake rococo with an oriental tang. One enters a vast marbled entrance hall and passes shops, banks and an advertisement for the Crazy Paris striptease show, before taking an escalator to an even bigger subterranean series of noisy smoke-filled rooms, all crowded with gamblers who drift from table to table or gather in crowds around some particularly large game with higher stakes than anywhere else. Some of the participants are surprisingly animated; others have a desperately stern, hunted appearance or seem hypnotised by the drama around them. Cameras are not allowed, and there are obvious patrols of heavyweight security men.

The entire proceedings are monitored by banks of special video cameras which are set high in the walls and record the betting process in a distant control room. The necessity for such precautions is simply proved by the astronomical figures of the cash which changes hands. Every year about 2.5 billion Hong Kong dollars are gambled in the five STDM casinos in Macao. Gambling employs one in ten of the local workforce and contributes fifty per cent of the government's revenue. The figures are so big that it is as if the entire population of south east England were to cross to a series of casinos in, say, Boulogne several times a year and gamble the equivalent of the budget of the National Health Service.

STDM has also tried to attract tourists to Macao with Portuguese and comic bull fights, women wrestlers, Thai boxing displays and the Macao Grand Prix. For some reason, it is difficult to discover the company's annual profit. When I asked Mr Ho, he said he wished he could tell me, but the government would not allow him to disclose the figure. He would merely say that his profit was 'substantial' and that I had better ask the government.

Eventually I asked Mr Antonio Pinho, the former head of the Macao Gambling Commission, a young and talkative Portuguese expatriate who was shortly to return home and who was not exactly enjoying his posting to Macao. He was more forthcoming, and told me that STDM contributed $600 million a year to the Macao government, and that Stanley Ho probably made as much as this himself. He mentioned that STDM often paid the air fares and hotel bills of certain gambling guests from Thailand and the Phillipines, but these clients first had to agree to buy a minimum number of chips. The Macao government did its best, he said, to control what he called 'the bad element' or traditional 'Triad' groups, and he admitted that some of the gambling operations in Macao were under the control of these Triads. He also revealed that the authorities were concerned about loan sharks and prostitution in the casinos of STDM.

When I asked Mr Ho about the problem of loan sharks in his casinos, he said that it didn't bother him very much because 'to be honest they are helping people to lose more money through the casino'. 'We don't like them when they use illegal ways or very drastic steps, like taking away peoples' passports,' he said, 'but otherwise it doesn't really bother us very much.' He said he had done nothing to keep loan sharks out of his casinos: 'How can I do anything against those loan sharks? . . . They are like gangsters and, being a merchant, how can we fight them? We can't. Only the government and the police can fight them.'

There was, he claimed, no particular problem in dealing with the Triads, since STDM controlled almost all the ferries and it was therefore a simple matter to collar undesirables as they tried to leave the colony. His explanation might not satisfy the more sceptical researcher into the truths of Macao's social make-up, but it was as far as Stanley Ho was willing to commit himself.

In the streets surrounding the main casino in Macao there are rows of pawn shops in which the most personal possessions of impoverished gamblers are displayed. Watches and wedding rings by the hundred are witness to the desperation of those who have needed to buy a ticket for one of Mr Ho's homeward ferries. When I asked him whether he was concerned that some people had been broken by their weakness for gambling, Mr Ho conceded that it did sometimes worry him. 'But I have given them sufficient warning,' he told me, 'I have put up notices in all the casinos warning them not to gamble heavily and only to gamble what they think they can afford, and to look at the whole thing as pleasure.' I wondered whether he might be worried when he saw that so many of his customers had had to pawn even their wedding rings in the pawn shops around his casinos. 'Well, these shops are licensed by the government,' he said, 'and I can't stop them from getting premises around my casinos, but I can assure you that there are no pawn shops in my complex.' He admitted that the existence of the pawn shops was worrying, but pointed out that it was difficult to control such things and that, in any case, pawn shops had been in existence in Macao for more than a hundred years.

Another response which I found surprising was Mr Ho's answer to a question about what qualities he looks for in senior managers for his casino businesses. ICI's Sir John Harvey-Jones had spoken of toughness and an ability to express oneself and get on with others. What Mr Ho is looking for in the senior casino managers is a more straightforward quality: 'They've got to be good in mathematics, because in the casino business mathematics has a lot to do with our operation.' I put it to him that what he really meant was an ability to count. 'Yes, counting,' he conceded.

It is obvious that much of Mr Ho's life is also spent in much the same activity, and I wondered what he did when he wanted to relax. 'To be honest with you,' he said, 'at the age of forty to forty-five I was still 190 lb with a big tummy, and I suffered from back pains. All that was because I could not find the time to exercise. I was striving very hard to achieve my goals. No exercise whatever up to the age of forty-two.' After the doctors warned him that he had to take some exercise, he took up swimming, tennis and shooting snipe, which he likes very much. He now goes swimming almost every day like a 'military routine': whether it is rain or shine one can see him in the pool, except when there is a typhoon. Swimming, the doctor had advised him, was the best exercise: 'Mind you, swimming alone is not much fun, I can tell you. But for me it's now like a military operation.'

One cannot avoid the impression that Stanley Ho is, in spite of – or perhaps because of – his riches, a lonely man anyway. It is not that he has an austere or remote relationship with his staff: in fact, from what we were able to observe, relationships in the huge block of offices where the affairs of many of his companies are administered are friendly, open and straightforward, with none of the bowing and scraping which might have been expected at the top of such a vast enterprise. In his private life he does not, however, appear to have a circle of close friends.

Tall and very slim, Stanley Ho certainly does not look his age, and now expends considerable effort in preserving his figure. There are many wrinkles round his eyes, but his features do not reveal what, if any, emotion is stirring beneath the cool exterior. His voice is quiet and low: he never seems to raise it, and he has a deliberate, almost bird-like manner of moving. He gives the impression of being a shy, careful man who takes pains to find the perfect solution to any problem and is always extremely courteous. His dress is correct and conservative, and it would be easy to pass him on a London street without guessing that he was a trillionaire.

Most of his homelife is spent in a large single storey house at Repulse Bay in Hong Kong, high above the teeming city and well shielded by security precautions: huge automatically controlled gates, high walls, fences and voracious-sounding dogs somewhere out of sight. The house is adorned with collections of jade and Chinese carvings and furniture arranged as if in displays not intended to be used. In the garage there are three Rolls Royces and at least two Mercedes. Across the lawns and fountains, a stone patio overlooks the swimming pool, flanked on one side by a huge aquarium in which prodigiously barbed tropical fish waft their way through exquisite fronds as if in some James Bond film – *The Man with the Golden Gun* was in fact filmed in one of Stanley Ho's floating casinos. Mr Ho sometimes takes a frugal breakfast on the patio in a dressing gown after his compulsory morning bathe, and often holds business meetings at the same time or signs piles of papers brought by a silent member of his staff. He has another house, of course, in Macao, but it is not so imposing as the Repulse Bay property, although it too is surrounded by security, and video cameras above the front door record all visitors.

Mr Ho has two wives, which is apparently still perfectly

acceptable in old Chinese circles. The first Mrs Ho, Clementina, suffered injuries in a car crash in Portugal in 1982, in which their only son and daughter-in-law were killed. The second Mrs Ho, whom we did not meet, is called Lucina and lives in Hong Kong. Mr Ho has three daughters but the family is now scattered. 'My children have never had to fight for anything themselves,' he told me, 'they have everything they want and they are not very much of a success'. This surprising comment was not a casual aside, but was delivered on the record during an interview.

Mr Ho's Macao house is even more crammed with jade and ornate furniture than the Hong Kong residence. It is the home of Clementina Ho, who whiles away her time looking after Rose Sarah, their grandaughter, the orphan daughter of their son, Robert. The Hos' three daughters, Jane Francis, Angela and Deborah, all seem to circulate between New York, the Bahamas, Switzerland and, sometimes, Hong Kong and Macao. It would be difficult to describe the family as being very close. Although the tragedy of losing an only son has undoubtedly left a deep wound, it is apparently simply never mentioned.

Stanley Ho is obviously aware that there are many who disapprove of the foundations on which his empire has been built. When I asked him whether he had ever had any satisfaction from making millions of dollars from the weaknesses of others, he paused, and then repeated that he had always had an ambition to make money himself, had subsidised the local government and economy, had generated employment and had always supported good causes. He worked so hard, he said, that he obviously deserved a little of the profit himself, but gave a great deal back in charity: 'I think that when you take it from people you have to give some of it back.' It was, he implied, not his fault if people were rash enough to gamble more than they could afford and ignore the warnings he had put up in all his casinos. It may, of course, be a simple case of poor observation, but on two non-gambling inspections of Macao's casinos I was unable to find any of these warning notices: perhaps like the health warnings on a packet of cigarettes they merge into the background.

His justification for his pride in his constantly increasing gambling profits is his record in giving to charity. He is certainly a renowned local benefactor, and in his office there are more than fifty different plaques which have been presented to him in recognition of some glorious work or other for which he has paid. At the University of Hong Kong, for instance, there is a Stanley Ho athletics track, and in Macao he has made an even bigger educational donation towards the University of East Asia, where he and the Governor were both recently awarded honorary degrees. He says that he is always being pestered by the backers of various good causes, and it seems that he has listened sympathetically to many requests for help.

On the walls of his Hong Kong house, among all the scrolls and framed awards, there is even a warrant from Buckingham Palace recording the gratitude of the Duke of Edinburgh for Mr Ho's gift of nearly £400,000 to the RAF Museum at Hendon in North London. Part of the money has been used to build a mock-up of an Operations Room in an exhibit to commemorate the Battle of Britain in 1940; the rest was spent on an extension to the museum and earned its donor a plaque, a hand-printed memorial book and his own specially named aircraft exhibit. He was, I understand, impressed by this formal acknowledgement and seems to have a genuine regard for Britain. At the opening ceremony at the RAF Museum in Hendon, he even gave a passionately patriotic speech which was so enthusiastic that it quite startled some of those on the same platform. He told me that he liked the British, had always felt grateful to them for the liberation of Hong Kong and thought that they had always treated him fairly.

Most of Mr Ho's charitable works have been undertaken in Macao, and they cover a wide variety of interests. He has, for example, spent $450,000 on the restoration of a local painting, *The Martyrs of Nagasaki*, which commemorates the execution of twenty-three Franciscan monks by the Japanese Shogun in 1597 and is displayed in a derelict seminary inhabited by a solitary bearded Jesuit priest called Father Teixeira. The priest, who came to Macao from an isolated village in Northern

Portugal when he was twelve years old, told me that Mr Ho had given three million dollars to the Catholic Church in Macao, even though he himself is a Buddhist. He has also helped other religious groups and charities. 'You see, everyone begs off him,' the priest explained, 'When a football team wants to go to Tokyo for a game, they have to ask him, or if schoolboys want to go to Malacca. They all go to him because he is a great benefactor, and it is better to use money for good than to do evil.' Father Teixeira was eager to deny any suggestion that Mr Ho's gifts were aimed at deflecting possible local criticism of STDM's casino activities. He described Stanley Ho as the economic ruler of Macao, and claimed that without the casinos the people of Macao 'would hardly live'.

The Macao Latin American Dancing Championships – Mr Ho is a devoted admirer and an accomplished performer – were held recently in the Lisboa Hotel, with the Governor and his wife as guests of honour. The entire cost, including the expenses of fifty competitors flown in from as far away as Britain, Australia and Japan, was borne by Stanley Ho. All the time, of course, while the dancers performed in the Lisboa's main ballroom and the guests were being lavishly entertained, the casinos in the rooms directly beneath the occasion were busily coining more Ho millions.

Many business enterprises in Hong Kong have recently experienced a period of uncertainty while the transfer of Hong Kong's sovereignty was being negotiated under the 1984 Sino-British agreement, which stipulates that sovereignty will change in 1997 and guarantees fifty years of capitalism thereafter. Since 1976, Peking has regarded Macao as Chinese territory temporarily under Portuguese administration. This formula seems to have suited both sides well, but there are murmurings from time to time that Macao has merely been left behind by history and that the Hong Kong agreement will be an ideal blueprint for Macao sometime in the future. None of the uncertainty appears to have ruffled Stanley Ho's business confidence. On the contrary, he told me that he was consider-ing withdrawing from some of his more far-flung enterprises to concentrate more of his investment nearer home.

I asked him whether his Macao operation could still be

profitable if, when the franchise bid next comes up in 1991, the government stipulates that the gambling tax should be not thirty but fifty per cent. 'That is going to be extremely difficult,' he said, 'My answer to you now is that I would say cheerio and good luck.' I put it to him that under the terms of the franchise he would then lose all the casino buildings. Did he really mean that he would give up? 'I'll tell you the reason. I have a casino venture in Portugal and another in Spain. From the one in Spain we are giving about twenty-five per cent, and we are not making any money already. The one in Portugal has to give about thirty-one per cent and, again, we are hardly making any money. So I don't think that in the casino business you can afford to give fifty per cent.' There were, he thought, at present enough casinos in Macao, and he claims that if he is granted the next franchise he has no plans to build more.

His sights are, it seems, therefore set on other lucrative possibilities. 'I think there is a very good future for real estate development in Hong Kong,' he told me, 'because ever since this Sino-British agreement, you'll find a lot of Americans, Australians and Japanese coming into the market trying to play level with the British. They know the British are not going to be here forever, and they have a chance now to compete on an even basis.' He thought that he would be able to take advantage of a change in circumstances, because all the new people would need the sort of assistance he could offer: 'They will want managers because they don't know the market. They may have money, they may have know-how, but they don't know the market. And we do. We know how to sell it to them.'

In spite of his protestations of affection, Mr Ho has what appear to be mixed emotions about Britain. On the one hand, he can make emotional speeches of great patriotism at the RAF Museum in Hendon, but at the same time he thinks that much of the success of Hong Kong is 'because we do not provide so much social welfare for the people'. He was quick to point out that there was help for the sick and the elderly, but said that the young had to fend for themselves: 'If you don't work here in Hong Kong, you starve. Our success is because it's unlike UK on a Friday afternoon, where the City is empty and everybody goes out to enjoy themselves.' If employers are willing to pay enough, people will work for them in Hong Kong on Saturdays or Sundays, he declared. In his opinion, people in Britain do not work hard enough. Because of social welfare, he claimed, they just apply for subsidies without work. 'You don't find any strikes in Hong Kong,' he claimed, 'I am very much in favour of the Conservative Government and I think you are doing a very good job fighting against these strikes, and I wish UK all the luck.' There was more slightly back-handed praise for Britain: 'You are much better now with deliveries, by the way – at one time your deliveries were very unreliable – and I have been also trying to help to buy more and more UK equipment. I think, given time, UK could be as successful as Hong Kong.'

What, I asked him, would happen to STDM when the time came for him to leave? Did he have a successor in mind? He said he did not believe in a man being indispensable and was sure that there would be someone to take over when the time came, but he still considered himself a relatively young man with a few more years of running the casinos.

When I asked him what effect China's take-over might have on his interests, he said that there was only a small possibility that he might have to leave the colony: 'Hopefully, if the situation remains more or less the same in China now, I think they're in the right direction and they are sincere in keeping Hong Kong as a capitalist society for another fifty years. Mind you, we are born and bred here, and would like to stay on. We know all the people here and it is so different if you have to start in a new country. But, just the same, in the event of an emergency, of course my first choice will be UK, because I could at least speak English better than any other foreign language.'

The Chinese, he claimed, had promised that the casinos could continue, and he was sure that the Chinese people would want to go on gambling: 'It's in their blood, let's face it. The Chinese love to gamble.' I asked him if he ever gambled himself: 'No, I don't, because I've learned that, after all, you never win – I mean it's a house game. Then I don't have the time. I work so hard – you have seen what I do. I like tennis, I like swimming and I really don't have the time or the patience.'

I put it to him that I had heard a local Chinese saying that Stanley Ho did not mind if one won at his casinos as long as one came back. 'That's very true, very true,' he agreed, 'As long as you come back, then I think you will all give it back to me.'

In Macao, and in many other places around the world, people are still trying to give it back to Stanley Ho, and are likely to continue doing so for a good many more years. He has more than fulfilled his promise to his mother, who probably would have had difficulty imagining just how he was to do so. Would she, one cannot help wondering, have approved, or would she have felt that the stigma of the pawn shop still lingered, even though those whose wedding rings have had to pay gambling debts and ferry fares have brought misfortune on themselves? All his material success and his outward cheerfulness have failed to insure Stanley Ho against tragedy in his private life, and although his undoubted generosity has brought considerable pleasure or comfort to many and has eased his own conscience, he still seems compelled to prove again and again that, unlike his father, he is a success. Having enough money, however it has been made, to give it away lavishly, is for him perhaps proof enough, and merely making money has become a habit.

RUSSI MODY OF **TATA** STEEL

CHAPTER 6

INDIA'S MAN OF STEEL

None of the other industrialists in this series is quite like the subject of the last of our portraits, Mr Russi Mody, the head of Tata Steel in India. None is so talkative or so sympathetic, none has such a bulky silhouette or regularly eats a twelve-egg omelette for breakfast; no-one else is quite so adept at card tricks or, as far as I know, bridge; the others do not, at the age of sixty-eight, still pilot their company's twin-engined aircraft or play the piano and sing night club songs they learned on the French Riviera, or recount how at Oxford University they once accompanied Einstein, the well known mathematician and less well known amateur violinist. Russi Mody can, and does boast of all of these talents. What makes him even more remarkable is that in the middle of Bihar, the poorest state in India, he runs the most profitable manufacturing industry in the whole of the sub-continent, and although he has often been enticed by promotion offers to go abroad, says he wants to stay in Jamshedpur doing what he can for the people he knows best.

In the state of Bihar, the newly arrived visitor is overwhelmed by the extent of poverty on every side. A crush of noisy humanity crowds the closely packed streets of the outer suburbs surrounding Jamshedpur; bullock carts, motor scooters, bicycles and rickshaws choke the potholed main roads; there are hordes of children wherever one looks; only a short distance from the tarred roads, dirt lanes lead into a network of impoverished villages with more barefoot children; women spread manure on the fields to dry, and their men drive carts or herd animals if they can afford to own them.

There are huge areas of territory in Bihar where law and order, and much else, have completely broken down, and where the chances of development have melted away in a mixture of corruption, apathy and bureaucracy. There is widespread poverty, illiteracy and disease, compounded by a booming population. It is therefore all the more suprising that it should be the setting for India's most successful private industry. From hundreds of villages in the centre of the state, it is possible to see in the distance the belching chimneys and blast furnaces of the Jamshedpur steel works. Without the wealth and jobs generated by the works, it would be difficult to imagine how many of the communities around here could survive at all.

The Tata Steel Company, or Tisco as it is usually called, was formed in 1907, part of a huge industrial complex run by the Tata family of Bombay with branches all over India. Other Tata firms make trucks, buses and trains, and generate power, but all depend on the success of the steel works in the middle of Bihar. In the early 1900s Jamshedpur was dense jungle – clearing the ground was hazardous, and there are stories of labourers being trampled by elephants and eaten by tigers. Now there are no fewer than 27,000 workers there, about four times the number needed to produce the same amount of steel in Japan. Many of them work with machinery which has been operating at the Jamshedpur works for more than fifty years. That it is lovingly maintained and worked flat out at minimum cost is one of the secrets of the company's success. Walking through the vast Dickensian sheds, one sees rows of elderly rolling mills and stamping and cutting machines glinting in the few shafts of sunlight which have somehow managed to penetrate the clouds of dust and steam; hordes of workers in tattered clothing, many of them shod only in flip-flops or sandals, fetch and carry alarmingly near passageways of molten metal. They work an eight-hour shift, sometimes six days a week, for a minimum daily wage of eighteen rupees – about one pound sterling.

Russi Mody appears to know every inch of the factory. He drives around the site in his white Toyota – he has the privilege, rare in India, of owning a foreign car – and, as our fearless guide, took us to see not only some of the most modern recently installed steel-making equipment, but also to the construction site for a new bar and rod mill, where hundreds of women labourers were carrying baskets of earth on their heads, and to blast furnaces and rolling mills where the activity was so furious and the noise so loud that conversation was impossible.

His squat figure is recognised everywhere. As he approaches, surrounded by a great crowd of officials, the workers draw aside and bow a respectful greeting, palms together. Sometimes one of them will try to lobby him during his progression: Mr Mody has the reputation of being the sort of manager who is at least willing to listen to anyone who wants to raise a point. He makes a quick decision, tells one of his entourage to make sure that something is done, or deflects a complaint with a smile or joke. Then he scurries to the next shed on his tour of inspection, sometimes making if difficult for his entourage to keep up with the pace he has set. He has long been used to the exercising of power, a characteristic which was forged early in his upbringing.

Rustomji Hormusji Mody – Russi for short – was born in Bombay in January 1918, the eldest son of Sir Homi Mody, a wealthy Parsi, who decided to send his son to Harrow public school in Britain.The young Russi Mody was, by his own account, deeply influenced by the experience of a British education, which he felt had moulded his life: 'All my thinking and my attitude towards others, my way of life, everything has been influenced by the years I spent in Britain. One particular aspect which I've had engrained in me as a result of my British education, I feel, is a sense of justice and fair play. I think I have found that terribly important in life, especially in dealing with people in India.'

Although he enjoyed his schooling, it could not possibly be compared with his subsequent three years as an under-graduate at Oxford, which he described as 'sheer heaven'. After the confinement of an English public school, he explained, he suddenly experienced the liberty to do whatever he wanted, to go to a lecture or not as he wanted and, apart from weekly tutorials, he admits that he only went to two or three lectures during his whole time at Oxford. 'I had a damn good time, and all on father's money, not my own,' he told me gleefully. 'I didn't have to earn that to have a good time, and apart from the six-monthly telephone calls from India, when father would admonish me for my extravagance, the rest of the time was great.' During one of the parental telephone checks, he told me, he complained to his father that he had no idea where his next meal was coming from: 'Father was very alarmed and asked in horror what I meant. I told him I wasn't quite sure whether it was coming from the Ritz or the Savoy.'

Russi Mody remembers, with pleasure verging perhaps on nostalgia, an enjoyably dilettante life at Christ Church, Oxford, where he rapidly established a reputation as a card player and a gourmet – his substantial breakfasts were legendary – and he was also known as an enthusiastic night club pianist. He formed a large number of friendships, 'saw how other people lived', and, although he found it difficult to explain, felt that: 'Every day I spent was in itself an education without my realising it.'

At one time, he told us, Albert Einstein was staying in the room next to his: 'We used to meet in the baths every morning. I used to be an early riser, and so was he, and he invited me one day to have strawberries and cream with him. He said "I occasionally hear the tinkling of a piano in your room – do you play the piano?" I said "Yes, I do try to." And he said "Why don't we have a duet? I will play the violin and you will play the piano." ' During the six months of Einstein's stay, Russi Mody told me, he must have spent at least twenty or thirty evenings with him: 'The greatness of the man was that after the first one or two occasions, when you could not forget that you were in the presence of possibly one of the greatest men in the world, he was really a very extraordinarily humble and ordinary person – when he was not doing nuclear physics.'

After Oxford, Russi Mody went back to India, where his father arranged for him to start work at Tata Steel, in the most junior post. It was, he admits, a difficult transition, but he managed to perform his duties satisfactorily even in the most menial positions, and as a result came to have an understanding of workers' problems which he could not have acquired in any other way. He did not, however, spend long gaining this sort of experience and was soon on the promotional ladder: he was not only well connected, but had also already established a reputation for earning the respect of the men he managed. By 1944, he had been loaned to the Tisco Controller's office to supervise the movement and purchase of coal for the war effort, and five years later he was promoted to a position as an Assistant Director in the Personnel Department in Jamshedpur.

Today, forty years later, his name as head of the company is known throughout India; wherever he goes on official visits in the countryside he is garlanded and treated with near veneration; he has a private pilot's licence and likes to fly himself in one of the company's twin-engined aircraft – an exhilarating experience for the passengers, who are no doubt relieved to notice that nowadays there is also a full-time professional pilot in the cockpit. A loose fitting safari suit disguises his girth: even his most effusive public relations man admits that Russi Mody has 'a bit of a tummy'. His build is in any case short and stocky, with broad shoulders and strong hands but surprisingly dainty feet: at home, he often slouches around in sandals. He speaks quickly, with an elegant accent which seems to be poised half way between Harrow and Delhi, and has a wide smile, slightly protruding teeth and an infectious laugh. But one is always aware of his reputation for bursting into a sudden towering rage if some trifle displeases him, and equally swiftly resuming his normal self when the crisis has passed. Although his pockets are never cluttered with pens and notebooks, he seems very attached to an ornate retractable gold tooth pick. He wears glasses and loves reading, and likes to drive himself around Jamshedpur in his white Japanese car at speeds which often alarm the inhabitants: woe betide the driver of any overcrowded bus which does not give way to the head of Tata Steel.

Russi Mody has a large and elegant single storey house in a quiet street in one of Jamshedpur's more well-to-do sections. It has a swimming pool which the British Royal party once used while on a visit to the town, and is approached along a broad gravel drive, between luxurious flowers and a cool lawn which need frequent watering. Women in flowing dresses lean over long switches of twigs as they unobtrusively sweep away the leaves. Inside the house, the atmosphere is elegant and restrained, with wood panelling and hand-coloured prints depicting life under Imperial rule. A comprehensive library includes a selection of modern best-sellers and a set of framed family photographs. After a particularly gruelling day, Mr Mody's retreat is a sitting room with low lighting in the centre of the house, where he plays his favourite Cole Porter or Rodgers and Hammerstein numbers on a grand piano.

His marriage to his cousin, Siloo, in 1950, was short-lived: the relationship soon came under intolerable strain, and the couple separated in the sixties. There were no children. As a gourmet – some of his friends say gourmand – Russi Mody likes to indulge his culinary passions by diving into the kitchens at his home, and cooking for himself and for anyone else who happens to be there. He starts by strapping an apron about his girth and ordering a gang of servants to bring him all the ingredients and utensils he needs. For our benefit, he demonstrated the preparation of a Parsi dish called Akuri: first he browned some onions and chillies in butter, then he whisked eggs in a shallow pan, all the time issuing a stream of instructions to his attendants. After he had spent some time fiddling with the gas, the whole concoction was at last progressing to his satisfaction and needed only the addition of turmeric, garlic and lime. He served his scrambled delicacy with hot toast, fussing round the table to make sure his guests had exactly what they wanted and could all pronounce themselves delighted with the results: I can testify that it was the most delicious breakfast I could imagine.

When Russi Mody travels to Europe, he likes to live in suitable style, and through directorships in London and Paris always has access to fast cars. 'What is the speed limit on motorways in Britain?' he asked us – although one suspects that he really should have known. He is a frequent visitor to Delhi and often sees the Indian Prime Minister, Mr Rajiv Ghandi, with whom he shares a passionate interest in flying. After a recent meeting to talk about the future of India's economy, the Prime Minister made a single note on the pad in front of him – 'Russi's jet' – to remind himself that Mr Mody had asked for government approval for enough foreign currency to buy Tata an executive jet. 'It will save me so much time,' Mr Mody told me.

When I asked him how he saw his present role in the company, he described how he would like to have 'maximum production, maximum profits, maximum happiness for the people who work here'. Above all, he said, he wanted to train sufficient numbers of people so that when he was gone, the company would not miss him. He thought that if he could genuinely do all of these things, he would have more than fulfilled his role in the company. 'I'm very keen that the company should be filled with young people, eager to take this company forward,' he declared. 'I want all the people down the line, even the poorest person, to want to do things differently from what he has been doing. I don't want to give a sweeper a vacuum cleaner – but I want the sweeper to say "I want a vacuum cleaner", then I'll give it to him. When that change of attitude takes place in my company, we shall be ready to march with the Prime Minister into the twenty-first century.'

His feelings about the way people come up to him on his progressions around the countryside and put garlands round his neck are mixed: 'It's an Indian custom – I would say a very pleasant custom. It's a nice way of greeting a person.' One garland he considers 'great' – but when it comes to 300, 400 or 500, as often happens, not only is his neck sore the next day, but he also considers it 'an awful waste of money': 'Each garland costs an enormous amount these days. The white ones with a silver thing thrown round sometimes cost thirty rupees each, whereas the marigold ones will probably cost only about a rupee or two.' He told me that he would much prefer all the money spent on garlands to be collected and given to one family, and has calculated that on his birthday, which is regularly attended by between 8000 and 10,000 people, he is given anything up to 6000 garlands, which he sends to the hospital. Shops are set up outside his garden for the sale of garlands, and he suggested that if all those who sold them were to put the money into a box, the contents would be enough for one poor family to live on very comfortably for a whole year. He has, he told me, protested many times about the numbers of garlands given to him, but with no effect.

'Nobody listens,' he said sadly, 'the habit is too well ingrained and, after all, you can't change everything in life – much as one would want to.'

Mr Mody need not be so modest. There may well be much more for him to do, but a great deal has already been achieved. Jamshedpur, the company steel town where he has spent most of his life, is noticeably more prosperous than other towns in Bihar. The streets, of course, are just as noisy, and are always filled with crowds of cyclists and scooter rickshaws; there are cattle wandering loose and beggars asleep in the shade; but compared with the rest of the state, Jamshedpur is rich, orderly, spacious and well laid out.

The town is named after the founder of the Tata group, Jamsetji Nusserwanji Tata, who made his first fortune by selling cloth to General Napier's British Expeditionary Force to Abbysinia in 1868. He built a cotton mill in Nagpur in central India, where the cotton came from, and soon repaid his investors handsomely. His immense bronze statue now towers like some Buddha over the main gate of Tata Steel. At dawn, when a niagara of workers pours into the plant, cleaners can be seen sweeping the statue, washing its bronze or garlanding it with flowers for special occasions, while bicycles clatter past its feet through the early morning smells and smoke.

Tata Steel has good reason to revere its extraordinary founder. In 1907 he went to London in an attempt to raise capital for his new venture – a steel works in the Empire – but was told that it would be impossible to manufacture steel in India. He was therefore forced to raise all the money needed from 8000 investors at home in Bombay, an event of great national pride. The Chairman of the Railway Board, Sir Frederick Upcott, was not impressed. 'Do you mean to say that Tata's propose to make steel rail to British specifications? I will eat every pound of steel rail they produce,' he promised. It is presumed in Jamshedpur that Sir Frederick must have died from indigestion some time ago.

J.R.D. Tata, a distant cousin of the founder, took over Tata Steel and eventually became the most famous of the whole Tata family. Like his predecessors in the enterprise, Jamsetji, Ratan, Dorab and Ratanji Tata, he was a brilliant entrepeneur, and he continued the group's policy of supporting universities, museums and other liberal causes which had so far been ignored by India's emerging industries. J.R.D. Tata founded Air India, had the first Indian flying licence and was still piloting his own aircraft at the age of eighty-two. It was he who, after an unbroken reign of forty-six years, in 1984 eventually handed over the running of Tata Steel to Russi Mody. Mr Mody could not fail to be conscious of being part of a long and distinguished industrial tradition.

As we drove with him to inspect the plant, vast clouds of sulphrous brown smoke were belching from the blast furnace chimneys nearby, in just the same way as the chimneys of Port Talbot or Dorman and Long used to darken the skies over Britain. If Tata Steel had to observe the same standards of pollution control as in Europe – regulations which have sometimes helped to kill the steel businesses which were once Mr Mody's competitors – and if the workforce at Jamshedpur had to conform to strict safety procedures and wear protective clothing, Tata Steel might perhaps not be able to compete quite so easily. As in many other fields, it is possible that the local tolerance of pollution in Bihar could be the factor which has lowered costs, seduced business from European firms and helped to close them. The whole matter is, of course, a very sensitive question for Indians; in characteristic form, however, Mr Russi Mody decided to fight back when I put the proposition to him.

His friends, he said, had advised him not to talk about pollution in our interview, because of his 'archaic views on the subject'. I pressed him by asking whether in India jobs were more important than considerations of the environment, which perhaps mattered more to Europeans than it did to Indians. 'I think there can be no two opinions that ecology has come to play a very important part in our lives,' he said. 'The realisation that it does play an important part is something that I welcome. Pollution control is something that I welcome. The only point that arises is that it has to be total. If I were to completely eliminate pollution from my company, it would cost anything up to 100 million dollars. I'm prepared to spend that, provided that Jamshedpur is pollution free. But pollution comes from the stoves that are being lit each evening – and we don't have smokeless stoves. We have no control over the cars, buses and taxis which ply in this town belching forth the most abominable fumes, which are very bad for human consumption. So all I would be able to do for a 100 million dollars is to perhaps reduce the pollution in this town without eliminating it.'

The steel works at Jamshedpur emit a pall of smoke and gas which wafts an orange and brown haze a distance of perhaps fifty miles downwind and could hardly be compared with the exhaust fumes of a few vehicles, but Mr Mody warmed to his argument. The question which now arose, he said, was whether, in a poor country like India, with such a dearth of hospital facilities, medicines and doctors, his $100 million could not be more usefully employed if he were, for example, to put up five or ten first-class hospitals managed by good doctors: 'Would that not do more good than merely reducing the pollution in Jamshedpur? I ask myself that question – I haven't got a complete answer for it – but I would not just go blindly on saying that pollution must be controlled because it's being controlled in America, England and every-where else. The poverty in this country is so vast that I think a great deal requires to be done on earth before we go into the heavens.'

Tata Steel has in fact already opened numerous clinics and hospitals, and has a public health record which compares favourably with most other industries in India. Nevertheless, there were, I suggested, people in the steel industry in Britain, for instance, who argued that it was only because Mr Mody was able to run a steel works on low rates of pay, with old machinery and little reinvestment, and without adequate safety and pollution controls, that Tata Steel had been so successful and had at the same time wiped out much of the European steel industry. He was unrepentant: 'Quite frankly, there are a thousand reasons given for failure, and I suppose you can equally as well give a thousand reasons for success, but ultimately what matters is the result.' In July 1985 Tisco announced quadrupled net profits of more than $68 million and sales were up by twenty-four per cent.

Another possible reason for Mr Mody's success is the fact

that his company owns its own resources of iron ore and coal within a manageable distance from the Jamshedpur blast furnaces. We saw him in action when he flew – as a passenger – to the open-cast mines at West Bokaro. On the journey, he played frantic games of bridge with his colleagues: he invariably wins, but not because the others are trying to flatter him. One of the skills he learned in his dilettante youth was how to confound opponents with the most cunning varieties of card tricks, and his bridge merely seems to be an extension of this art: his repertoire of card tricks is dazzling, and he seems to take a childish delight in his audience's amazement.

When the aircraft rumbled to a halt on the dirt strip at Bokaro, there was an official welcoming party, with the inevitable garlanding of the Chief, while a crowd chanted slogans in his honour. We were taken for a tour of inspection in a caravan of elderly Ambassador taxis along potholed roads to a village where there was a Tisco-sponsored birth control clinic. More and more garlands were heaped on the neck which would suffer the next morning. There were so many people he had to greet, so many officials trying to catch his attention and, all around, a great and excitable crush of young children: it seemed as if three quarters of the population must be under the age of twelve. There were presentations and songs and speeches of welcome; one could not help thinking that the government of India in its offices in Delhi was a very long way away.

On the way back from the excursion, our caravan was stopped by a group of people standing in the road and waving black flags on poles. It was a demonstration by local villagers to protest to Mr Mody about the way Tisco had expanded its open-cast coal mining without compensating local farmers for the land they had lost. The open-cast coal mine at West Bokara is a vast pit about a mile across. At one side of the crater's lip is a roadway of black sludge, down which a string of huge American-built dumper trucks drive in convoy. Deep down at the lower levels, a giant excavator loads boulders and rock spill onto the dumpers, which then very slowly grind their way to the outer edge of the crater and disappear. Mr Mody did not get out of his car to speak to the demonstrators, but promised that he would see what could be done, and then drove off at speed for tea on the rough grass of the company guest-house lawn, where a different set of supplicants – this time middle management – wanted to raise other matters.

A tour by a provincial administrator in the time of the Raj must have felt very much like this, with a jeep and armed police in attendance; turbanned waiters in almost white uniforms silently arranged table-cloths. In the background the world's longest aerial ropeway clanked its buckets of coal from the distant mine to the distant railway at a rate, we were told, of 2.5 million tonnes a year. In the guest house, there was a video which, when the power supply allowed, showed an hour-long programme of the company's celebrations on Russi Mody's appointment as the first new Chairman for forty-six years. On the screen one could see vast crowds holding placards with slogans like 'Welcome to our glorious Chairman'. They had waited for hours in the heat, we were told, and had then had to listen to the new man delivering his speech in Hindi, which was clearly not the language in which he was most at ease. Some of the senior managers seemed to find it all rather amusing. While the seemingly interminable film was being reshown, its hero was relaxing at the dinner table, demonstrating his skill with cards. If he should ever tire of a career in industry, he could be snapped up as a TV conjuror. I watched, hypnotised, as new packs were broken open and shuffled by expert hands. Mr Mody's eyes suddenly become inscrutable as he peers through his thick spectacle lenses and asks his victim to choose a card: you must not tell what it is, and it is, of course, only a matter of seconds before the card in question is palmed from some unlikely place, or appears as if by magic in another set of cards which you have been jealously guarding all the time. It is brilliant, stylish and incomprehensible – perhaps qualities for which Mr Mody would not mind being renowned himself. Outside, the aerial ropeway finally came to a halt – perhaps it had broken down again – and we could hear dogs barking in the surrounding villages under the moon.

I asked Mr Mody what were the difficulties of running a company in a state like Bihar where, as everyone knew, there were widespread problems with law and order. In Jamshedpur, he told me, there was never a problem with public order, but in the coal-mining regions of Bihar it was different, 'akin to Mafia rule': 'The whole of India recognises it. You can only deal with it when the Mafia chieftains are not affiliated to various important politicians in this country. They have their patrons in high places in government. You ask any law and order officer, and he'll tell you he can clean up the place in a week. The very fact that they are not doing it, is an indication that the people who say they would like to clean it up are not really capable of doing it because of reasons other than the exercise of law.'

In a small but significant sector of Bihar, Mr Mody said, there was absolute anarchy. As an example, he described an incident at one of the company's collieries some time before: the clerks were all at work at eleven o'clock in the morning, when 'One fellow came, stood opposite the desk of one of my clerks, and shot him dead. He quietly walked back to his car.' Although the number and description must have been taken by all the people around, nobody has ever been apprehended. This sort of thing was happening all over the place all the time, he told me. 'We just carry on as best we can and treat it as an incident, but it is not an incident,' he maintained angrily, 'it's symptomatic of a malaise which has gone very deep in that part of the state. It is an anarchic state of affairs, and India is not an anarchy. India is, by and large, well governed, considering the magnitude of its problems and the size of its population. I think the law and order situation in this country is, by and large, good. We happen to be living in a good part, whereas the mines happen to be in a bad part.'

Tata Steel has somehow managed to insulate itself from the worst of the local disorders. One possible reason is the company's unique co-operation between management and unions. In the worst administered state in the country, where trade unions have often been undisciplined and sometimes even criminal, Tisco has the remarkable record of not having had a single strike for more than fifty years. There are many factors which could help to explain such an amicable arrangement, and most concern Russi Mody and his genius at getting on with his workforce: it is an ability which is widely recognised and which is regularly demonstrated at mass meetings.

His principle management technique is to hold regular meetings, at which eventually every member of the staff has a chance to raise any grievance. Most of the meetings are followed by a vast tea in the open air, where it is possible to spot Mr Mody's bulky figure in the crowd and lobby him by elbowing through the ranks. I saw a couple of such meetings: selected questioners were invited to step up to the microphone and deliver their points in public. It takes a courageous man to challenge the Chairman on the platform, and there were several occasions when I felt that Mr Mody seemed to take pleasure in scoring points off the poor unfortunate who had dared to raise some concern which he did not think very important. On the other hand, the men themselves speak of these contacts very positively and want them to continue.

'Dealing with people and their wants is a continuous non-stop job, and the sheer boredom of it is somehow difficult to cope with,' Mr Mody confided. 'But to each individual who comes to me with a problem, to him it is the most important thing in the world, and he probably has this one opportunity, which he may not get for another year or two, of being able to come and communicate with me. So I have to be very careful that even though the answer may be no, he doesn't leave my presence with any sort of bitterness besides the disappointment of not getting an affirmative reply.' When I asked how he managed to achieve this, Mr Mody explained that he always asked a man to sit down and join him with a cup of tea: 'I talk to him, I try to explain to him why his particular request cannot be met. The reasons for not meeting it are not because I don't want to help him, but because of various repercussions that might take place by doing so.' He explained that he always followed a visit with a personal letter, which he signed himself, so that the man should 'feel a little better that his complaint was not, shall I say, dealt with very casually'.

The Tata Workers' Union is one of the oldest trade unions in India. It had a turbulent beginning in the early 1920s when a bitter and prolonged strike was only finally resolved by the intervention of Ghandi himself. Ghandi managed to persuade the Tata managers that instead of ignoring the Union, they should recognise it. An agreement in 1948 stipulated that new joint committees should be formed, with equal representation, 'to ensure better understanding and the settlement of disputes by joint negotiations'. Conflict had been deliberately replaced by conciliation.

The President of the Indian National Metal Workers Federation, Mr V.G. Gopal, a small hunched man with pebble glasses and a hearing aid, offered us tea in his offices in Jamshedpur and, surprisingly, a detailed analysis of recent manoeuvrings in the TUC in Britain. He said that he had known Mr Mody for thirty years, and had always thought him a very dynamic person, but considered him at the same time a compassionate man who wanted to stamp out injustice and did not allow fraud or indiscipline. Why had there not been a strike at Tata Steel since 1928, I asked. 'Both management and union have realised that a fight is not the ultimate thing,' he said. 'If we can find ways by which disputes can be discussed without undue delay, them there is no need for a strike. If we ask for reasonable things, the management cannot deny them and we, the union, also felt that we should not ask for things which are unreasonable and create a situation in which there could be confrontation.'

The most extraordinary result of this unusual management and union partnership came when the Janata Government tried to nationalise Tata Steel in 1979. The General Secretary of the Janata Party, George Fernandes, India's Ministry of Industry from 1977 until 1979, told me that he had invited Tata to a meeting in Delhi at which nationalisation was put to the company. The board was told that it would be in India's interests if Tata were to give the whole steel industry the benefit of the company's unique experience in management and profit-making. Mr Fernanades claims that the Tata Steel managers heard him very politely, but then left his offices and organised a passionate and expensive propaganda campaign against him. He even went to Jamshedpur himself, he said, and tried to explain to the workers what the nationalisation plan meant, but was met by a 'black flag' demonstration and roughly handled. Russi Mody, he claims, rushed forward 'with tremendous concern for my safety and asked whether I wanted the police to help me'. Mr Fernandes rejoined that he had handled crowds before and was capable of handling a crowd again – even one which in effect had, he claimed, been organised by Russi Mody himself.

Both Mr Mody and Mr Gopal dispute this version of events, but it is clear that beneath the smooth exterior of Tata Steel's labour relations there are powerful forces at work. Mr Fernandes does not feel he has any reason to love Tata, and claims that the management organised the demonstration: 'Mr Mody wanted to teach the Minister of Industry a lesson: that you can't possibly brow-beat the Tatas.' Mr Mody told us that he wished he had been able to organise the demonstration against nationalisation, because it would have proved that he had more influence than anyone thought possible; but, he insisted, he did not organise it, and it was ridiculous to imagine that organising demonstrations was part of his job.

It is certainly true, however, that Tatas have no particular regard for the state-owned steel sector in India. Mr Mody claims that in the private sector he is a servant who is left alone to do his job, and says that this could not possibly happen if his firm were nationalised. He pointed to SAIL, India's national-ised steel industry, which was five times as big as Tisco, and claimed that its management had been ruined by constant political interference: SAIL was, in his opinion, hopelessly inefficient. He expected to die at the age of ninety, Mr Mody told us, but if he should instead close his eyes for good at about the age of eighty, it would be entirely due to frustration of dealing with Indian bureacracy: 'By that I mean that every time I have contact with the bureacracy, the sheer exasperation which I face is, I'm certain, shortening my life.'

Until recently, Russi Mody was planning to retire even-tually to Britain, where he still has many close connections and where he would never be too far from the diversions of the French Riviera, which he had loved so much in his youth – and, one suspects, considerably more recently – but he now sees his future as inextricably tied to the base of Jamshedpur and to his friends in Bombay and Bihar. He still keeps a close and sympathetic eye on affairs in Britain, where he has often found developments worrying. 'I feel sad at times for what it was and what it is,' he told me. 'I don't mean sad at the loss of Empire. I never did have much use for the Empire as it stood at that time, and certainly not for the Indian Empire.'

'This Commonwealth concept' which had taken the place of the Empire was, he thought, in a way an even stronger bond, 'a bond of real friendship and a community of ideas'; its strength lay in the fact that it had been entered into voluntarily and not under force. At the same time, he said, he was sad that as a result the people of Britain had such a high rate of unemployment and that their industries were not functioning as they should. 'I think there has been a general deterioration of standards everywhere,' he generalised, continuing in a style which would have delighted any high Tory audience in the shires: 'All this has come about as a result of the march of events. The world has moved on, and values that you and I enjoyed in our youth no longer predominate. Values about morality, sex, everything, have changed.' He claimed to welcome, rather than to deplore, this inexorable march of time and its accompanying change in attitudes. 'In a way there has been a considerable liberalisation of our ideas,' he asserted, 'and many people object to that. I don't personally; I think it's a healthy trend.'

He was not, he assured us, trying to argue that this was responsible for Britain's industrial decline. Instead he thought that it was the result of the latitude and freedom with which the Trades Union Congress was allowed to rule England: 'If I may be blunt, I think there was a period when the TUC really ran things the way they saw it and wanted it, and while I am no – shall I say – opponent of the Trade Union Movement, and in my own country would certainly be considered as a friend of labour, I do feel that things had gone too far and that the TUC were getting more and more selfish. They wouldn't see the scene as a whole, they wouldn't see what was good for Britain.'

His reply to my question about why he thought that Britain had not been more successful industrially was crisp, although the argument was a familiar one: the wage increases that had been acquired for the workers by the unions had been too easily conceded, without a corresponding responsibility on the part of the British worker to give a return for what he was getting. 'In fact,' he claimed, 'I think that the work ethic in Britain was allowed to slip. Discipline was not what it should have been, and the unions, by and large, were allowed to taste power and pretty well dominated things, in my opinion, to the detriment of the industrial climate in Britain.' In that case, I asked, where would he put the blame, on unions or on management? 'I always blame governments rather than the TUC,' he replied, 'I would blame the management rather than the workers in every sphere of life. If there is a lack of leadership, then it leads to the kind of situation you found in Britain.'

When I asked him where he would identify the lack of leadership, he said that it always had to start from the top, from the Prime Minister: which, somewhat paradoxically, was why he was an admirer of Mrs Thatcher, because under her 'things are improving in Britain, in my opinion'. Although he admitted that Britain's unemployment rate was high, he claimed that 'Everywhere else there is a realisation that had Mrs Thatcher not come in and tried to do what she is doing, Britain would have reached a point of no return from the slippage that was taking place.' Mrs Thatcher, for that very reason if for no other, had, he said, already done 'a magnificent job' for Britain.

I wondered whether he realised that there were people in Britain who might not completely agree with his analysis of the Prime Minster's role, especially as he appeared to condone an authoritarian and dictatorial approach: 'I'm quite certain that because of her style of management and all that goes with a personality like hers, she cannot be a reasonable person and expect to be able to do the things she does. Reasonable people cannot do that. The person who leads, the person who's enforcing his or her views on a situation that needs to be corrected, cannot be the normal type of person amenable to reason, having a lot of common sense, a sense of judgement: all these things take second place.' There might even be Thatcherite supporters who would take issue with the implication that their leader had dispensed with reason, common sense and judgement, although he added hastily: 'I'm not saying that they're completely absent, but they take second place to the desire for making that change, and that can only come from a strong and determined leadership.'

It sounded as if he was talking about a dictatorship, I suggested. 'Not necessarily. There are many people who, when they assert leadership, are prepared to subordinate their entire democratic ideals to the need of the hour, without actually turning a democracy into a dictatorship,' he explained, 'Mrs Thatcher is aware, as I'm sure other strong leaders before her were, that ultimately the electorate is supreme, and so long as that realisation is there you cannot have a dictatorship – but you can certainly have strong leadership, which must not be mixed up with dictatorship.'

Mr Mody obviously has a soft spot for firm government. In the light of his remarks about the influence of trade unions, I wondered how he would explain why so much of the British steel industry had bitten the dust at a time when the Indian industry seemed to be continually expanding. His answer was not so much a political analysis as a technical and economic explanation. Steel works had been closing not only in Britain, but even in America, Germany and Japan, he said. A United Nations agency had predicted that by the end of the century the world requirement for steel would be 800 million tonnes. It was unfortunate that every country had what seemed to be a craze for producing more and more steel, almost as an index of its omnipotence in world affairs. 'They already have 700 million tonnes capacity only fifteen years away from the century,' he pointed out. So, as there was 'an over-capacity installation of steel . . . when the recession came, it got hit harder than any other, and you had to cut it down'. There were other contributory factors in Britain, he added: 'Mind you, in Britain you had to cut down to a large extent also because of the overmanning of the various steel plants and the antiquated machines and technology that you had, which just could not compete in cost with the more modern technologies of Japan and the Continent, even.'

In India, things were very different, he pointed out. Whereas some countries used steel at the rate of 700 kilos per person per year, in India, which was a developing country, the figure was only 15 kilos, yet there were more than 700 million people committed to development and industrialisation, for which steel was 'a very important input': it would be in short supply well before the end of the century. Lower labour costs were only one factor in the way the Indian steel industry was able to compete on the international market, and Mr Mody said that he could see no sign of there being a recession in steel in India for some years. He told me that the steel works at Jamshedpur had always worked at 100 per cent of its 'capacity utilisation', and said that he did not believe that a poor country like India could afford the luxury of buying the equipment to produce 100 tonnes, and then only producing 70 tonnes from it.

This, he told me, was one of the reasons why the public sector was not performing as well as he would have liked. 'Quite frankly this idea of the public sector is quite stupid,' he said, 'It's no more public than I am, in the sense that the public sector is made up with my money. In taxes and in other ways, I have invested in the public sector and I want my investment to flourish.' When I asked Mr Mody why the state steel enterprise, SAIL, should be less efficient than Tata Steel, he insisted that it was not the fault of the people who ran the public sector: 'We Indians come from the same background, the same educational institutions; we get roughly the same wages. The men in the public sector are as good as, or in some cases better than, the men in my own company.' It was rather, as we had been told by other industrialists in other countries, a question of freedom: 'The systems under which I operate and the managing director of a public enterprise operates are vastly different. On paper perhaps he has wider powers than I have – on paper. But it is not allowed for those powers to be exercised, because of certain circumstances inherent in the system.'

The accountability to Parliament of the Minister in charge of the steel industry was, he said, the starting point of what he termed 'the malaise' within the state system: 'He feels he must get all kinds of the most irrelevant information to filter up to him. He feels there is nothing wrong in his interfering.' It was the compulsion to be accountable to Parliament, along with the interference from the Ministry, which he saw as the basic difference: although it was always denied that the Minister often decided who should be appointed in what job, and who should get a contract where, this was nevertheless what happened. Mr Mody thought, however, that under the new Prime Minister such practices had received a 'very severe jolt'. The new Chairman of SAIL, who had come to the job with an enormously successful track record from a heavy electrical firm and from Maruti, the new car company, would, he was sure, be able to do a good job, provided he was not distracted by political interference.

In Delhi, the head of India's nationalised steel industry, Mr Krishnamurthy, could not have been more complimentary about Russi Mody's abilities. ' A great industrial leader, a very colourful personality, a legendary figure, an aristocrat every inch who at the same time has the greatest consideration for the human beings who live and work with him', were some of the personal descriptions he gave me. 'He will never contemplate doing anything which is judged to be wrong by society or by the country; I do not think he would consciously do anything that is against the law or against the interests of the people in the country.' When I asked with suprise whether this was not the case with all industries, Mr Krishnamurthy replied: 'There are not very many people like that in this country. He is very committed to his work, and for a man of his eminence and of his attainments he could have taken many other important positions and have moved into government and even been a Minister, but no, he stayed at Tata for more than forty years, and, brick by brick, he helped to build that organisation until he was the proud Chief Executive of perhaps the most successful industrial enterprise in this country.'

The secret of Tata Steel's success, according to Mr Krishnamurthy, was Mr Mody's continuity of service, his ability to show concern for the workforce and to lay greater emphasis on human than on material resources. The result was that the employees were committed to the organisation and considered him to be their leader: 'Anything that he said should be done is done immediately.' Mr Krishnamurthy admitted that the state enterprise in India did not work in quite the same way. He had not been in the job for long, and agreed that one of the biggest defects of the state system was the fact that no Chief Executive ever stayed in the position for more than two years, but he did not agree that all the top appointments were made for political considerations. One of the problems he saw was rather that staff were shunted around from place to place, which made commitment to the organisation less marked and the task of team building more difficult within the short span of their term of office.

When I asked why a private company was able to do more good works for its employees than a state enterprise, he pointed out that nationalised companies had tried similar schemes, but said that there was a 'touch of class' in what Tisco has done: 'You must grant it to the house of Tatas for having done this job exceedingly well.' The fact that a private-enterprise, profit-oriented organisation had shown so much concern for the people who lived in and around Jamshedpur was something 'remarkably good', he declared, 'That's what makes Tatas great.' He told me how, when he had first taken up his post, Mr Mody had come to see him with much useful advice about what could be done to improve the nationalised industry's poor performance, and said that he was very grateful for this kindness.

Since he was such a respected giver of economic advice, I asked Mr Mody what sort of a relationship he had with the Prime Minister, Mr Rajiv Gandhi. 'I know him and he knows me,' he replied, 'I was, shall I say, closer to his mother – and I certainly belong to an older generation than Rajiv. I don't know what he thinks of me, but I have a tremendous admiration for him, and there is very little in the world I would not do if he were to ask me.' Mr Mody continued his eulogy by describing the Prime Minister as a saviour of India: 'I honestly think he has appeared on the scene at the right moment. He has a Herculean task before him and he's making all the right noises. But I want those noises to penetrate first to his own party and secondly through to the bureacracy. If and when that happens – and all of us must pitch in with him to make the same sounds so that the passage through the various layers is easier – I think there is a great future for this country with his type of thinking.

He's modern, he's enthusiastic, he doesn't believe in precedents and the past and things like that. The good traditions he will keep . . . the bad practices that have grown up over the years he will, I am sure, be able to brush aside.'

Mr Mody's admiration for political leadership was a distinct contrast to the perspectives of an Agnelli or Harvey-Jones. I wondered whether he differed from them in other ways, such as over their views about priorities in the choosing of management, and asked him what qualities he looked for in selecting senior colleagues. 'First and foremost,' Mr Mody replied, 'I look for character. That, of course, encompasses integrity, credibility, a certain amount of compassion, certainly courage – all these are attributes of what I would call character. Certainly I wouldn't take a senior manager who is a fool. A certain amount of intelligence would have to go with it and ability. But if I had one post and only two people were available, a terribly able and clever man and a man who had all the attributes of character such as I've mentioned, I think I would choose the man with the character in preference to the able man – I would choose the attributes of character rather than the attributes of mind.' He did not mention toughness, as Sir John had done, nor an ability to add up, Mr Ho's chief requirement.

Mr Mody likes to give the impression that he is most at home in the simple life of unsophisticated Jamshedpur among the people he knows best. It is true that he is now firmly rooted there. Every time he returns, he performs a private ritual of driving to the cemetery and standing in front of his mother's grave to say a prayer. He is obviously deeply attached to his house, servants, books and the slightly out-of-tune piano on which he can sometimes be tempted to play songs of the 1930s and 1940s with a vocal accompaniment in tolerable French: his rendering of 'J'attendrai' drew vigorous applause even from a Yorkshire cameraman and the rest of a usually unimpressionable film crew.

Even at the age of sixty-eight, however, Mr Mody is still an enthusiastic and compulsive traveller. Because of his business commitments he has to fly all over India – he is, among other things, Chairman of Indian Oxygen, Davy Ashmore and Tata

Incorporated, and a Director of Tata in London. Occasionally he still pilots a Beech Queen Air twin himself, but he is usually a passenger in one of the Tata aircraft while he plays bridge and gossips or plans – or does both – noisily and interminably with his companions. He sometimes visits the United States, travelling first class on scheduled airlines like Air India, but prefers London, Paris and the South of France. One gets the impression that although he is secretly proud of a misspent youth he would rather that not too many of his fellow countrymen should know of his visits to the Riviera and his familiarity with good restaurants.

'I am only hassled by the amount of travelling I have to do.' he told me, 'In the course of a month I have to be in Bombay for certainly one week, then Calcutta and Jamshedpur . . . I have to visit the two capitals of the states where I operate. Then there are my own mines and collieries, which I visit once in a while, so all in all, for about fifteen to twenty days a month I am in the air. That does, at the age of sixty-eight, impose a slight strain. If I could get myself a jet aircraft I would certainly find it easier – anything that flies faster than the 250 mph I am flying around the country at the moment. If I could add another 200 mph I would not be very particular about what sort of plane I got.'

Mr Mody clearly has the experience and negotiating skills which would allow him to work anywhere he liked, but he has resolutely opposed all attempts to move him to the company's head office or anywhere else. In spite of his continuous travel, he is now firmly based in Bihar: the career which started with Harrow and an Oxford History degree is committed to the affairs of a small provincial industrial town which has become an island of comparative wealth in the ocean of overwhelming poverty outside its walls. There Mr Mody is the only authority which counts.

When I asked him what it was that kept him in India, his answer was immediate: 'Basically a desire to do something for my country. I love the poor people of my country. Whatever frustrations I have are with, shall I say, the educated classes.' On a lower level, he liked Indian food, and as his mother and father had been Indian and had brought him up in India, he therefore could not leave the country: he felt 'very comfortable' there. 'I'm not a rich man,' he told me, 'but my company provides me with a large amount of comfort and I'm quite happy, especially as I have an opportunity to go abroad on work at least two or three times every year. And that gives me diversity of environment, which I appreciate.'

I asked him whether there was any contradiction in saying that he loved the poor people while at the same time he was clearly living a life which was so much more affluent than anything they could ever dream of. 'I don't see the connection between my own life-style and my love for the poor people,' he protested. 'I don't think I'd help a single poor person in this country if I were to suddenly start saying that I would live the same life as he's living. I don't think anyone gets helped like that. On the contrary, if I could help somebody a peg or two up, rather than myself down, I would prefer that. I think that's the right thing to do: it's better to pull people up than to pull people down.'

One could, he told me, do a lot of good from a position of authority and power: he enjoys both at the present moment and is able to translate his views about 'how poor people should be treated and how they should be dealt with and how they should be communicated with' into practical form. To be in a position to do that gives him 'an awful lot of satisfaction': 'It's not a question of lording it over other people – that's a menial sort of authority and power – but power to do good, the power to give a decision, the power to say "Do this" is, in my opinion, a very important element of power if properly used. And I thoroughly enjoy doing it.' No one who has ever met this extraordinary man would disagree with that.

Mr Russi Mody is, in many ways, the most interesting of the industrialists we met on our grand tour. This is not so much because of the environment in which he works (although for a westerner that obviously imbues everything about him with a sense of unique and exotic novelty), as because of his skill in inspiring loyalty in his workers, in settling disputes and in encouraging his colleagues at all levels to aim for the same goals. The other industrialists we met also have these skills, but to a lesser degree. In Russi Mody's presence, one is always aware of his abilities as a manipulator par excellence – which is by no means to say that he is insincere. Although he is rich by the standards of Bihar, he does not do what he does for material rewards, however welcome these may be, nor even for the good he might do to the impoverished local community – although this is a genuine objective – nor for national recognition, which he already has. He might not like to admit it, but his ultimate satisfaction seems perhaps to come simply from charming others into agreeing with him. Although he claims never to have read a book on management in his life, he has nevertheless turned himself instinctively into a supreme manager of men.

CONCLUSION

We chose the six businessmen for this series of portraits from the widest spectrum; three from the West, with experience of chemicals, cars and oil; three from the East with an interest in electronics, steel and in what one might call the service industries. There could have been many other permutations with other sets of equally significant and interesting personalities but this one, we thought, would encompass the more important industries and articulate men who had a vision beyond their particular fields.

It is, of course, tempting to look for similarities of character, background, temperament and opportunity as a possible key to their common success. But one of the factors which makes them interesting is that they do not fit conveniently into moulds; in fact, part of the very reason for their success is that none is in the mould business.

There are, however, certain obvious characteristics which all share, and which all seem to be proud to exhibit – stamina and dedication or, to borrow Sir John Harvey-Jones' word, toughness. It is not that each consciously chooses to be tough, or to become dedicated to the business he lives for. It is that these characteristics seem to have come to all of the naturally. They are inborn.

Many of the attitudes to business which our 'money makers' have been prepared to reveal, particularly the parables of Japanese management technique, are lessons which others might learn and practise if they wished. In themselves, the examples cannot produce a guaranteed winning formula; only the touch of secret genius does that. But in the end genius in business may not be the rare commodity we are led to believe. In many of us, perhaps, it is simply waiting for the chance of expression.